"Idols of the heart
God, Dennis New
them in the blazing glory of God's greatness."

—Dr. Daniel L. Akin, president,
Southeastern Baptist Theological Seminary,
Wake Forest, North Carolina

"Have you as a Christ-follower ever considered yourself to be an idolater? Well get ready. Dennis Newkirk will allow you to see yourself. And you might be challenged with what you see. But keep reading. You are about to take a new and deep journey in your walk with the Lord."

—Dr. Ted Kersh, senior pastor,
South Tulsa Baptist Church, Tulsa, Oklahoma

"This is a powerful work that will challenge every believer—the newly converted and the seasoned saint. Its mandate, skillfully presented, is crystal clear: identify your idols and clean them out. Here is a book that will ignite—or reignite—your ministry....Most importantly, here is a book that will call you back to the love and intimacy you can and should enjoy with your Savior. Here is a book that will lovingly show you how."

—Dr. Michael G. Scales, president,
Nyack College and Alliance Theological Seminary,
Nyack, New York

"Most people don't want to hear a sermon about idolatry let alone read a book about it. Why? It might mean we have to get rid of some things we would rather hold on to....Dennis writes with a firm yet pastoral spirit that brings the reader face to face with the truth of Jonah 2:8, 'Those who cling to worthless idols forfeit the Grace that could be theirs.' By the end of this book, the reader will be ready to run to the 'idol bonfire.' Dennis makes it crystal clear that nothing in this world can compare with the joy of a 'God-first' life."

—Dr. Ronald Walborn, dean,
Alliance Theological Seminary, Nyack, New York

"*No gods but God* gets to the heart of the matter. At the foot of Sinai only forty days after hearing the one true God speak his covenant to them, the newly liberated Israelites abandoned God's first two commandments and fell into idolatry. Sadly, but perhaps not surprisingly, we too often fail in idolatrous ways no less tragic than constructing a golden calf. May God use Pastor Newkirk's timely book as a warning, a reminder, and an encouragement to put God first and follow him."

—Dr. David Wesley Whitlock, president,
Oklahoma Baptist University, Shawnee, Oklahoma

NO GODS BUT GOD

To Mimi
Towards having no gods but God
Denis [signature]

NO GODS BUT GOD

Confronting Our Modern-Day Idolatry

Dennis Newkirk

CROSSBOOKS

CrossBooks™
A Division of LifeWay
1663 Liberty Drive
Bloomington, IN 47403
www.crossbooks.com
Phone: 1-866-879-0502

Unless otherwise noted, all Scripture taken from The Holy Bible, English Standard Version. *Copyright © 2000; 2001 by Crossway Bibles, a division of Good News Publishers. Used by permission. All rights reserved.*

© 2012 Henderson Hills Baptist Church, Edmond, Oklahoma. All rights reserved.

No part of this book may be reproduced, stored in a retrieval system, or transmitted by any means without the written permission of the author.

First published by CrossBooks 11/13/2012

ISBN: 978-1-4627-2223-5 (sc)
ISBN: 978-1-4627-2221-1 (e)
ISBN: 978-1-4627-2222-8 (hc)

Library of Congress Control Number: 2012919511

Printed in the United States of America

This book is printed on acid-free paper.

Cover design: Lindsey Rae Robinson

Because of the dynamic nature of the Internet, any web addresses or links contained in this book may have changed since publication and may no longer be valid. The views expressed in this work are solely those of the author and do not necessarily reflect the views of the publisher, and the publisher hereby disclaims any responsibility for them.

Contents

Acknowledgements ix
Introduction xi
1. Interrupted Plans — 1
2. Idolater? Who, Me? — 13
3. Wake-Up Call — 31
4. Revelation — 55
5. Revelation Response — 71
6. Fellowship with the Father — 93
7. Called to Be a Disciple — 109
8. Peter's Pattern — 127
9. Changed Hearts; Changed Nation — 137
10. Final Thoughts — 149

Appendix: How Can I Have a Relationship with Jesus Christ? 155
Notes 159

Acknowledgements

I'm grateful to many people who have taken part in the process of creating this brief study. The Lord is the one who inspired it and enabled it to be written. My precious wife, Marcia, walked through these experiences with me and was always my counselor and support. My sons, Chuck, Kyle, and Chris, also walked through these days with me, and they encouraged me greatly. The people of Henderson Hills Baptist Church in Edmond, Oklahoma, blessed me by their surrender to God's Spirit. Keith Tracy, a member of Henderson Hills was essential to the process of creating this written document. Cindy Sheffield, also a member of the church and staff editor-writer, has played a vital role in editing this book.

Introduction

"Do you know what your problem is?" Every time someone has said that to me, I've found the ensuing discussion to be less than a happy one. Often it has been true, but it's still hard to hear. I don't like the question at all. Nevertheless, I start this book by asking, do you know what your problem is?

If you are a Christian, your problem is the same one that I and all other Christians have struggled with. It is the primary sin mentioned in the Old Testament and one often mentioned in the New Testament. I'll never forget what happened one summer when God revealed our problem—and this sin—in such an incredible way.

CHAPTER ONE

Interrupted Plans

I stood at the front of a room full of teens and their sponsors, not saying a word for what seemed like a very long time. My prepared notes were in front of me. They were biblical and organized in a logical fashion—the product of many hours of study and preparation. But I was unable to begin preaching.

It was the first night of our high school church summer camp, and I was privileged to be the camp pastor. As the senior pastor of our church, it was a rare treat to have a captive audience of teens. Plus, the thought of a respite from the Oklahoma summer heat to speak to our students at Silver Cliff Camp in the Colorado Rockies made it all the better. I was looking forward to the services and had planned a series of messages on discipleship.

Just a short time earlier as the service was starting, however, I had begun to feel uneasy. There was no obvious reason for my uneasiness. I've spoken at summer camps dozens of times, and I love to preach to students. Since these were teenagers from our own church, I was also quite comfortable around them.

As our worship leader led us in singing, the feeling persisted. It was similar to what you might feel when looking for an unfamiliar address and you begin to suspect something is not right, that you are driving the wrong direction. So instead of standing and joining in the singing, I remained seated, praying about what could be the cause of this unsettledness.

Then specific passages of Scripture began coming to mind. I sensed there might be a special significance to them, so I searched for something on which to write them down. I didn't have any blank paper, so I turned over the file folder that contained the week's carefully prepared notes and began writing.

The first sentence I jotted down was "Have no gods but God," along with the scripture Exodus 20:1–3. After writing four more sentences prompted by various verses about idolatry and obedience, but not sure what I was to do with them, I stood and joined in singing the last song. Then I stepped up to the lectern and opened my sermon notes.

Now here I was, standing in front of everyone like I had forgotten what I was supposed to say. The audience was oblivious to the internal struggle playing out in my mind and spirit. I simply was unable to pull my thoughts away from those five sentences and accompanying verses.

Have you ever read a passage of the Bible you've studied many times, but this time when you read it you could understand and apply it with so much deeper insight than ever before? That was what was happening to me as I stood there.

Finally, submitting to the overwhelming sense that God did not want me to preach from my notes on discipleship, I closed the folder. I turned it over to what I had written just a few minutes before, deciding for just this one night I would speak on the first sentence I had written down. I silently prayed that it was indeed a Spirit-inspired decision.

There was nothing special about the sermon. It wasn't theatrical or dramatic; I used no heart-wrenching illustrations. In fact, at camps I'm especially careful when talking to teenagers. I don't want them to make spiritual decisions in an emotionally charged environment that will not have any lasting impact on their lives once they board the bus and head home. I simply talked to them in a conversational tone for about twenty-five minutes, hoping these travel-weary students would gain something from the message. At the close, I asked them to pray about applying the principle to their lives.

I was about to dismiss the service when one of the students stood and asked if he could say something. Then he walked to the front of the room and stood beside me. He confessed he had allowed his heart to slip away from God, after other things, to other gods. He repented of the idolatry in his life, and we prayed for the young man.

Then another student came, and another, and still others. Some knelt at the front of the room to pray. Many came to share their testimonies, confess sins, ask for prayer, and receive Christ. That night's planned-to-be-short worship service—with an unexpected, unplanned message—lasted for over two and a half hours! I was exhausted but overjoyed at how I saw God working in these students' lives.

The next morning my wife, Marcia, and I rose early and headed to the dining hall for breakfast. We began to notice several small groups of students. As we drew closer to them, we realized the students were praying. Then we noticed groups were scattered all around the campground. The leaders hadn't scheduled a prayer time. The students were simply compelled to do so. That's when I realized how significant the night before was to the students.

Throughout the day, the leaders attempted to continue with the planned schedule. But over and over again, we saw students in personal prayer time or huddled in small groups praying. There was an electrifying change to the atmosphere. I sensed what I believe was a literal, manifested presence of the Lord permeating the campground. I felt like Moses walking on holy ground.

I continued to speak throughout the week from the principles God had impressed on me that first night. Over and over he convicted these teens about the idolatry that had stolen their hearts away from him. Word spread about what was happening, and attendance at our worship services grew each day. Camp workers and people who lived in nearby cabins joined us. News about what was happening at camp reached home, and before the end of the week some parents had traveled out to join us. By the last night of camp, the service was so full that some had to sit outside the building and listen through opened windows.

I'm convinced there is no way to describe what happened at Silver Cliff other than to call it a true revival. I have never experienced anything like it in all my years of ministry, and I was humbled to be a firsthand witness to one as it unfolded.

Even before we left the camp, we had started calling those simple—but very important—lessons God taught us about idolatry, obedience, and repentance the "Silver Cliff Covenant." Once home, the students recorded the covenant on a large poster and signed and framed it. They hung it in the youth area as a public testimony of their commitment to follow the principles and as a reminder of how God had turned an ordinary high school summer camp into a revival.

So what's the problem all Christians have? It is giving our attention and heart to other gods rather than God.

The Un-Campaign

Now fast-forward to about nine months later. I was on a study leave in Phoenix. I had planned to use the time to prepare my heart and sermons for the upcoming months, but my thoughts kept drifting to the plans being made by our staff back home.

They and the stewardship team were working diligently to prepare an upcoming capital fundraising program. They had kept me apprised of the campaign details and asked me to give a stewardship message at the kick-off banquet.

There was only one problem. A big one. I couldn't escape a troubling thought. I had prayed about it, discussed it with Marcia, and simply tried to ignore it, but still it persisted. I had the distinct impression God did not want us to proceed with the campaign plans. It made no sense to me. Why wouldn't he want us to proceed?

A few days later we returned to Oklahoma. Still I sensed we were to go no further with the campaign plans. It was déjà vu of the Silver Cliff experience. Once again it was internal struggle and interrupted plans. Instead of the stewardship message, which was the obvious topic for the banquet, I felt like God wanted me to talk about something else—a two-fold message, actually. The first part was intimately familiar: have no gods but God and keep yourselves from idols, which was the first principle he had given me at Silver Cliff. The second part was new, and I wasn't sure what it meant: get ready for what God is going to do.

The kick-off banquet, which was to be held the following Sunday evening, was now only days away. Logically, it made sense to give a message on stewardship, and I was hesitant to make an abrupt change in topics. Yet, I knew I had to be obedient about what was being impressed upon me. I wondered how I would tell the other staff about this, fully expecting them to think I had lost my senses.

A couple days later the pastoral staff gathered for our weekly staff meeting. We began with a few minutes of open sharing time. Without prompting, man after man began to describe what he thought was an unusual intervention of God's work in his life in recent days. Each concluded God was calling him to a much deeper walk with him—and to much deeper *fellowship* with him than ever before.

The Lord also revealed two specific verses to us that day. The first was 1 John 5:21, which says, "Little children, keep yourselves from idols." The second was Luke 12:54–56:

> [Jesus] also said to the crowds, "When you see a cloud rising in the west, you say at once, 'A shower is coming.' And so it happens. And when you see the south wind blowing, you say, 'There will be scorching heat,' and it happens. You hypocrites! You know how to interpret the appearance of earth and sky, but why do you not know how to interpret the present time?"

If I were to paraphrase what Jesus was telling the crowd, I'd say, "Listen, you guys. You're good at interpreting the signs of nature to forecast the weather, but you're not very good at seeing the spiritual signs. Look around you. Pay attention to what is happening. These are not coincidental experiences. I have been revealing my presence to you. I have been telling you to prepare your lives so you can prepare others."

All of us pastors felt like God was telling us the same thing. We needed to prepare ourselves to experience fully his manifestation and work among us so in turn we could prepare others. The second half of the new message for the stewardship banquet now began to make more sense to me. I had not yet expressed my conviction to halt the campaign plans and change the banquet message. Now I had an opening to do so, and I explained to the other pastors what I thought God was impressing on me.

We began to pray, seeking confirmation of God's will. I needed to know I wasn't alone in sensing this from God. Soon we knew without a doubt that the direction of the campaign had to be changed.

"We're supposed to be sharing on Sunday night about the next step for our church," one pastor said after we finished praying. "We thought we understood what that was. But now, what is the next step?" Admittedly, we were more than a little concerned about standing before a few hundred people at the banquet, now only four days away, and simply saying, "Get ready." There was a human expectation that something more was needed—an apprehension that this word from God wasn't enough. After all, it was a *stewardship* banquet. "It's not about money. It's about the Lord," said our worship and arts pastor. He was right.

God had gotten our attention. He clearly wanted our focus to be on him, with no obstacles hindering our worship and service. If we would examine what we were experiencing, we would have no doubt he was moving in our lives, and in the life of our church, and preparing us for a special time ahead.

The next evening the pastors sat down with the stewardship team. These men, who had generously dedicated their time, knowledge, and energies, had been meeting for months. They had prayed, studied, and prepared an excellent fundraising plan. I took a deep breath, apprehensive to begin but confident in what I had to say. I explained what we felt God wanted us to do.

Then I paused, waiting for the expected resistance to this unexpected about-face on my part. "God's been giving us the same impression," the men said. Unbelievable! Or was it? We pastors expelled the collective breath we had been holding. God was widening the circle of people to which he was revealing what he wanted.

The Stewardship Banquet

The following Sunday evening I stood before the congregation and talked about what it meant to have no gods but God—how we let modern-day idols steal our affections for God. I also told them how we felt God was leading us to get ready for him to do a mighty work among us.

I closed the message by explaining that since we had built some new buildings, we had a five-hundred-thousand-dollar annual debt payment. If we could pay it off, our general ministry fund could be released from the payment responsibility and made available for whatever ministry God was calling us to do. We encouraged the members to give to the building campaign fund—but only if they felt God's direction to do so.

I'll be honest; it was extremely difficult for us to obey the Lord in this. It actually was a frightening time. Satan taunted us with thoughts such as, "What if no one gives?" and "What if your congregation thinks you're crazy?" Nevertheless, I knew we had been obedient to God, and I tried to push aside these doubts and concentrate on trusting the Lord.

The next morning the office was full of chatter about the night before. Then the pastors began hearing from church members. They weren't telling us we were crazy; they were telling us about amazing things God was doing.

On Tuesday morning, I received an envelope with just my name on it. Inside was a very short note: "God spoke. He said this much." It wasn't signed, and inside were ten one-hundred-dollar bills. My first thought was, Wow! This much. My excitement grew as I saw that the person hadn't signed the note. By Thursday evening, almost sixty-one thousand dollars had been given, and each donation contained a note of similar testimony. The lasting significance was that God had spoken. I had done nothing except to extend a call to put God first and to be obedient to him. The fundraising effort from then on became known as the "un-campaign."

Strange Time of Ministry

The two verses God gave us earlier, "Little children, keep yourselves from idols" and the Luke passage about analyzing the present time, consumed my thoughts for several weeks. I'd go to bed thinking about those verses; I'd wake up in the morning thinking about those verses. I discussed them with my wife and the staff. God prodded me to dig deeper into these scriptures than I ever had before and, in turn, to preach on the insights about idolatry and obedience he was giving me.

The weeks immediately following the banquet seemed like one of the strangest times of ministry our church has ever seen. Just as God had interrupted my speaking plans at camp and before the banquet, it happened again and again. Many weeks I would find myself stepping behind the pulpit about to open my mouth to preach and then abruptly stopping, sensing the Lord's leadership to share from a different passage than what I had prepared.

I rarely preach "off the cuff" and only when I strongly sense the Lord is leading me to do so. But now I felt like my willingness to be obedient to God's promptings was being tested every single week. One of the many personal lessons God reinforced during this time was my need to totally depend on him to supply the messages that came out of my mouth. He repeatedly reminded me that I was completely inadequate to deliver sermons in my own strength.

Relationship and Fellowship

Often I have people ask me about how they can feel closer to God. They are disappointed and frustrated with their Christian life. They confess that they thought there would be more to it than what they were experiencing. After several years of a status-quo existence as a believer, for all intents and purposes they had given up believing it was possible for them to ever experience more.

Do you find yourself identifying much too closely with what I've just described? That after many years of being a Christian you too have resigned yourself to a so-so experience?

For our church, both Silver Cliff and the stewardship banquet served as wake-up calls and prologues to a time of much deeper learning about God's truths and growing closer to him. Both were very unique, special experiences that may never be duplicated in the life of our church.

In this book I want to share the lessons God taught us about idolatry, obedience, and serving. Ordinary people had their lives changed in an extraordinary way by an extraordinary God. People who had a disappointing relationship with God learned how to have a deeper, more intimate relationship with the Lord. It is possible for any of us.

When a person comes to a point of acknowledging being a sinner, confessing sin before God, believing Christ paid the penalty for believers' sin with his blood on the cross, and asking God to be Lord and Savior, the person now has an eternal relationship with Christ that cannot be taken away. This is a permanent relationship based on God's salvation, and that relationship will remain secure no matter what. Compare it to the familial relationship of a child to a father. It cannot change. In the same way, once a person is a child of God's, he or she is always a child of God's.

Relationship, however, can also refer to *fellowship*, which is our spiritual interaction with God or the God-to-man activities of a believer's Spirit-filled life. We commonly use relationship in this manner when speaking of the quality of two people's connection to one another. For example, we would use it in this way if we asked someone, "How's your relationship with your father (or boss, spouse, daughter)? Good? Bad? Strained? Close?" The relationship will vary in intensity or closeness depending on how we've cultivated it. When talking about this type of relationship, I'll use the term fellowship.

When Christians desire a closer relationship with God, what they're really seeking is more intimate, deeper fellowship with God the Father. Many of us may exhibit the symptoms of not having that close fellowship, such as a growing dissatisfaction, spiritual dryness, unanswered prayers, or feeling distant from God. Unfortunately, we don't understand the yet-unidentified cause.

We must discover the root issue that is creating the obstacle between God and us before close fellowship can be restored. It is vital to our spiritual health to become acutely aware of this cause-and-effect dynamic. When the Holy Spirit nudges us that something isn't quite right in our relationship, we would do well to stop and deal with the problem—and to do so quickly before it builds into a much greater obstacle. That's what God was calling us to do as a congregation, to examine our lives and see what obstacles were hindering our close fellowship with him. Our obstacle? Idolatry. Then God began to strip away our preconceived notions about it and worship.

Make no mistake. These were painful lessons, and not everyone wanted to venture down the path to experience them. I love our church and love that members were so openhearted to the Lord. Each week the other pastors and I would have someone stop and talk to us or write us, telling us what God was teaching them through the messages. They confessed how they had let their hearts slip away from God, which also meant they had lost the close fellowship we as believers were meant to enjoy with him. Not only did he change individual lives, he changed us corporately and solidified the direction of the church.

How God called our hearts back to him is the story that will unfold in the following chapters. First, we'll look at what modern idolatry is and why it is so offensive to him and harmful to us. Then we'll learn about the four-step pattern God uses to call our hearts back to him. Finally, we'll explore how as Christians we were created to enjoy a deep, intimate fellowship with our Creator God and to serve him.

Many of us have not connected idolatry to the things today that can draw our hearts away from God. What about you? Are you willing to admit you might be a modern-day idolater?

CHAPTER TWO

Idolater? Who, Me?

Some of you may argue that idol worship passed out of existence several centuries ago. Although you may concede that some religions and cults still engage in idol worship, you don't think twenty-first century Christians do. If you're one who believes that, this will be an interesting chapter for you.

Generally speaking, worship is the expression of admiration for something or someone and the dependence we place on that thing or person. We are all worshippers of something. The question is not *do* we worship, it is *what* do we worship? When we worship God, we give him the highest value, devotion, and desire of our lives. We express this through trust, praise, obedience, service, and other actions and attitudes that demonstrate he is our highest priority. Conversely, sin creates in us a desire to worship the created rather than the Creator. Taking the gifts he has given us and turning them into objects of our devotion is idolatry.

Money, power, and possessions are the obvious culprits of our modern-day idolatry. But look a little bit deeper and we will uncover many others. What about attitudes, people, relationships, and ideas, to name a few? The students at Silver Cliff seemed to quickly grasp the more subtle ones. I witnessed them confessing how girlfriends, boyfriends, sports accomplishments, music, and many other ordinary things had become idols for them.

In the weeks after the stewardship banquet, many church

members confessed they were guilty of turning things into idols. "We have gotten rid of the HBO idol in our home," one man wrote me. While that may not be an idol for everyone, for him it had become one and he decided to tear it down.

A woman wrote to tell me how God had touched her heart through the message. She had been saving to buy a particular item, but over the past couple months God had burdened her heart several times to release her savings for this thing she wanted. She now realized how she had stubbornly clung to the money rather than asking God how he wanted it used. She repented of making it an idol. "Once I asked God to forgive me, I had a wonderful peace down inside and in knowing that I was able to start over," she wrote.

She also enclosed a check for what she had saved so far—nine hundred dollars. Although it's impressive she would be obedient and send the check, it's more impressive that she had recognized a holy God present and calling to her.

Idolatry Defined

When we participate in idolatry, it creates a huge obstacle in the closeness of our fellowship with God. We feel the distance, but we don't often understand the reason for it. Part of the reason is that we don't fully understand what idolatry means today.

In ancient biblical times the word *idol* meant "a substitute god." Throughout the Bible we are told how the Israelites, God's chosen people, turned to idols crafted from wood, stone, and metal. They disobeyed God's explicit command to have no gods before him (Ex. 20; see also Matt. 22:37–38).

Furthermore, God repeatedly warned the Israelites not to associate with or marry pagan foreigners, knowing that if they did, they would be tempted to worship the foreigners' gods. Yet, time and time again the Israelites ignored his warnings while rationalizing that worship of other gods was somehow acceptable.

They engaged in conspicuous idol worship, setting up idols in their homes to worship and sometimes even displaying them in God's temple. It was disgusting to God and destructive to those who practiced it. "With their silver and gold [the Israelites] made idols for their own destruction" (Hosea 8:4).

Think also about the ancient Romans. They too were examples of blatant worshippers of the "created" rather than the Creator. We could list gods of light, healing, childbirth, agriculture, hunting, and truth, among many other things that they worshipped.

I know I can look around our church and not see any man-made statues like the idols primitive people worshipped, nor will I find any of them in our members' homes either. We may not worship pagan statues or the sun, but we Christians today are no less guilty of being idolaters than the people of the Bible. The *what* man worships has changed; the basic definition of idolatry has not.

Idolatry is the sin most addressed in the Bible—and not just in the Old Testament. Who was John's audience when he wrote "keep yourselves from idols" (1 John 5:21) and Paul's when he wrote "flee from idolatry" (1 Cor. 10:14)? Christians. Admittedly, these New Testament authors were warning the recipients of their letters about worshipping the pagan idols that were prevalent around them, but they were also addressing the heart issue of idolatry.

Several scholars offer additional thoughts that help us define it. Herbert Schlossberg writes:

> Idolatry in its larger meaning is properly understood as any substitution of what is created for the creator. People may worship nature, money, mankind, power, history, or social and political systems instead of the God who created them all. The New Testament writers, in particular, recognized that the relationship need not be explicitly one of cultic worship; a man can place anyone or anything at the top of his pyramid of values, and that is ultimately what he serves. The ultimacy of that service profoundly affects the way he lives. When the society around him also turns away from God to idols, it is an idolatrous society and therefore is heading for destruction.[1]

Additionally, Timothy Keller says:

> What is an idol? It is anything more important to you than God, anything that absorbs your heart and imagination more than God, anything you seek to give you what only God can give. A counterfeit god is anything so central and essential to your life that, should you lose it, your life would feel hardly worth living. An idol has such a controlling position in your heart that you can spend most of your passion and energy, your emotional and financial resources, on it without a second thought.... An idol is whatever you look at and say, in your heart of hearts, "If I have that, then I'll feel my life has meaning, then I'll know I have value, then I'll feel significant and secure."...If anything in life becomes more fundamental than God to your happiness, meaning in life, and identity, then it is an idol.[2]

And, finally, Richard Keyes says this about idolatry:
> An idol need not be a full-sized replacement for God, for nothing can be. We become increasingly attached to it until it comes between us and God, making God remote and His commandments irrelevant or unrealistically prohibitive. In this society, our idols tend to be in clusters. They are inflationary, have short shelf lives, and change, adapt, and multiply quickly as if by mitosis, or cell-division. An idol can be a physical object, a property, a person, an activity, a role, an institution, a hope, an image, an idea, a pleasure, a hero—anything that can substitute for God.[3]

Idolatry is not difficult to understand. When we let our hearts wander away from God, we turn to something else in his place. Sometimes we create our own idols by willfully disobeying God to follow after or to possess something or someone. Then our idolatry is deliberate and defiant. We not only let our hearts drift away; we are boldly at the helm and steering them the wrong direction.

Other times we engage in more passive idolatry. We succumb to it because we have not taken the steps to prevent our hearts from gradually slipping away from God. Nevertheless, idolatry is idolatry whether arrived at by aggressive or passive means.

Two-Part Idols

Substitute gods actually consist of two parts—one tangible and one intangible. For example, say I lust after a new car to the point it becomes an idol for me. The car is the tangible part of my worship. But the companion component of that idol is the underlying motivation—the intangible part. In this example, the intangible idol might be greed or the desire for status.

Another person may have allowed health and fitness to become idols. Her thoughts and time are excessively consumed with eating habits, weight loss, and exercise. Those are the tangible parts of the idols. But the intangible part might be the fear of advancing age or the fear that her husband someday won't find her attractive and will leave her.

Keyes says, "All idols come in pairs. One is always stronger than the other, and each one corresponds to the two directions of the human personality—dominion, now become domination, and trust, now become overdependence." He names them "nearby idols" and "faraway idols."[4] For example, someone might have a nearby idol of money. The other half of the pair, the faraway idol, might be the belief that financial security will bring happiness and provide immunity from aging and death.

Similarly, Keller calls idols "surface" and "deep" idols.[5] The deep idol is the heart issue at the root of the idol, and thus the heart must be changed before the idol can be abolished.

Unfortunately, as human beings—even regenerate ones, we seem to have an unlimited capacity to create substitutes for God. Our actions are first born of our thoughts, and at the root of our thoughts is our heart. John Calvin said, "Hence we may infer, that the human mind is, so to speak, a perpetual forge [factory] of idols.... The god whom man has thus conceived inwardly he attempts to embody outwardly. The mind, in this way, conceives the idol, and the hand gives it birth."[6]

The root of all idolatry can be traced back to heart issues, with greed and pride being two of the most dangerous. So although possessions, people, and power might be obvious replacements for God, we need to think about how our attitudes, emotions, and relationships can morph into idols too.

Another member wrote to me after the stewardship banquet saying this about an attitude idol:

> Thank you for the message last night. That's what I really needed to hear. Although I must admit that it was not the topic that I was expecting [me neither!], it was relevant to my spiritual condition. I have been allowing some idols, one in particular, to creep into my life.... Your message was so pointed at my situation that I had to deal with these issues and beg God's forgiveness and cleansing. Now what I really want to do is invest my life in helping prepare the way for the Lord and his coming among people.

What a wonderful testimony of conviction and a change of heart.

Desires Turned to Idols

John warns us about three worldly things God despises: desires of the flesh, desires of the eyes, and pride of life (1 John 2:16). The desires of the flesh refer to what makes us feel good. We pursue these simply because of the pleasure they bring. The desires of the eyes describe the things we see that lure us away from God, and the pride of life refers to whatever encourages us to put ourselves before God.

These desires could also be categorized a little bit differently: desire to be loved, to have security, to enjoy life's pleasures, and to be significant. Certainly not all idols can be neatly packaged into these categories, but I believe our lusts, or desires, lie at the root of our tangible idols. Underlying motives such as greed, pride, control, selfishness, overdependence, insecurity, and fear continually weave themselves through our basic desires.

Desire to Be Loved

Most people very much desire love. Unfortunately, people sometimes turn to unhealthy or sinful ways to try to earn love, such as engaging in a sexually promiscuous lifestyle, straying into adulterous affairs, or obsessively seeking approval from others to feel loved and to validate their self-worth. When they place a higher value on being loved by others, or what they perceive as being loved, than being loved by their heavenly Father, their pursuit of love relationships becomes idolatrous.

Loving and being loved by others is good. My wife, Marcia, and I have been married for more than forty years. I love her completely, and I feel completely loved by her. It is a glorious God-given blessing to be loved like that. But if either Marcia or I were to put our love for one another before our love for Christ and satisfaction with him, it would be wrong.

I remember a woman who came to talk to me about how miserable she was with life. She was intelligent, educated, funny, and a delightful person, but she was overwhelmed by loneliness. Her parents were both dead and she was an only child. She had a few casual friendships but longed for someone to love her. She felt like she was a complete failure in life because this basic need was not being met.

Actually, she was suffering from idolatry—the belief that her value was dependent on someone else. Her consuming desire was for a man to love her.

Do you remember the story of Jesus and the Samaritan woman at the well? Have you ever considered that their conversation was a confrontation about her idol? In John 4 we find the story.

Jesus was resting beside a well one day around noontime when a woman came to draw water. He started the conversation by asking her for a drink (which is a great example of how to seize an opportunity to engage people in spiritual conversations, by the way). I imagine this shocked the woman. Bitter antagonism existed between the Samaritans and Jews, and she was a Samaritan. A Jew would never stoop to ask a Samaritan for anything, and a Jewish man certainly would not speak to a Samaritan woman.

When Jesus asked her for a drink, the woman was caught off guard. She was probably both curious and suspicious about why he would make such a request. When Jesus explained he could offer "living water," in other words the Holy Spirit, that would permanently satisfy her thirst, the woman wanted it. At this point, she most likely was only thinking about what a relief it would be not to have to trudge back to this well every day carrying heavy water pots. She didn't really understand what his offer meant, but living water sounded like a great idea, and so she said, "Give it to me."

Then as if totally ignoring the present conversation, Jesus tells her to go get her husband. What?! It was an unexpected, confusing request. She probably stammered a moment as she explained she was single and had no husband, to which Jesus pointed out she was living with a man who was not her husband and that she had been previously married five times.

Why did Jesus tell her to go get her husband? To confront her with her idolatry and sin. To show her that her desire to be loved could never fully be satisfied by another human being. For Jesus to become her Lord and Savior, she needed to turn away from other gods and to him as her source of satisfaction and confidence.

If we first look for another person—a girlfriend, boyfriend, spouse, parent, or anyone else—to satisfy our desire for love, we will be disappointed. The best love relationship a believer can ever have is with our loving Father.

Desire to Have Security

If we let our fellowship with God become distant, one of the symptoms might be a loss of security. There is nothing wrong with wanting to feel secure, but if we turn to our own strengths and talents or to other people or things as the source of our security, we have replaced God-based security with false security. We may not even think we need God anymore. "When we are alienated from God, we search for enough security—from controlling some part of the world—so that God seems unnecessary,"[7] Keyes says.

People seek security in jobs, money, and relationships. Many people measure security by the amount of money they have in the bank, how large their retirement account is, or how well their investments are performing. Money helps them feel secure about their future. But unfortunately, wealth can be a relentless, controlling master.

In the Sermon on the Mount, Jesus introduced his disciples to what it means to be his follower: "No one can serve two masters, for either he will hate the one and love the other, or he will be devoted to the one and despise the other" (Matt. 6:24). Since slavery was common in the New Testament culture, this example made sense to his audience. They knew a slave was obliged to obey and follow after a single, full-time master with full-time obedience. It was not possible for the slave to serve two masters at the same time because if he tried, he would ignore one and follow the other. A slave's allegiance could not be divided.

The Greek word for "master" is *kyrios*, which is the same word that is often translated as "Lord" in other passages of Scripture. Read the verse again, this time substituting the word *lords* for *masters*. No one can serve two lords. We are created to be monotheistic worshippers.

At the end of the verse, Jesus brings home his point with a specific example: "You cannot serve God and money." (Some Bible translations interpret "money" as wealth or mammon.) The Greek word for *serve* is a present tense verb meaning "to serve and continue to serve." It means we cannot make a way of life by serving God and wealth. We cannot serve, or worship, both God and prosperity at the same time.

Another time an unnamed, young man approached Jesus with a question, "What must I do to inherit eternal life?" (Luke 18:18). Jesus first mentioned a few of the commandments—specifically five of the last six, which have to do with our relationships and actions with others. The rich, young ruler proudly proclaimed he had kept them all.

Then Jesus, who knows our hearts and motives, shifted to the topic of the first four commandments: idolatry. He told the man to sell his possessions and give the proceeds to the poor. But because the man put such value and trust in money and the objects it can buy, he turned away and walked off the pages of Scripture, still clutching his god of money.

We must continually take stock of our lives. What value do we give our possessions and money? Are we willing to disobey God to earn more money? Will we forgo time with the Lord to try to make more of it? Do we put our trust in it to keep us safe, secure, and happy? Do we spend too many hours working to earn more money and neglect our family? If we do, we've made money a substitute god and put our trust in something that can only give temporary security.

Desire to Enjoy Life's Pleasures

Some people live as if life is all about feeling good, enjoying certain comforts, avoiding pain, seeking an escape, buying the latest toys, or being entertained. They are pleasure- and comfort-seekers. One commentator says,

> Pleasure-seeking destroys the spiritual faculties. It is not required that the Christian should be an ascetic, denying himself innocent delights, nor is it to be supposed that all pleasures are evil. The evil is the love of pleasure. Even the love of pleasures that are innocent in themselves may be the rock on which a soul is ruined, if this be the supreme passion of that soul, eclipsing the love of God.[8]

Unhealthy obsession for pleasure can lead to the pain of serious addictions and health ailments. For example, making food or drink an idol can lead to obesity, alcoholism, or related diseases. Gambling, excessive shopping, and drugs may offer fleeting thrills but can quickly turn to addictions. When we take sex out of marriage and pursue it strictly for pleasure, we have disobeyed God's command

and made it an idol. Pornography is another example. When pleasure controls us, we have become its slave and it our idol.

All kinds of pleasurable things can become idols. A new car, house, or boat. The other day I spotted a young lady driving a very nice pickup truck with the license tag "MY1STLUV." Many of us act that way about our things, though we may not proclaim it so publicly.

Sports, hobbies, television, and friends can become idols. So can the latest cell phone, most powerful computer, newest game console, or other just-released technological gadget. These things promise to make our lives easier and us happier. When the time-consuming activities technology affords us—such as texting, tweeting, social networking, and online gaming—consume too much of our time and thoughts, they are no longer serving us but we are serving them.

Desire to Have Significance

Lastly, we can create an idol of our quest for significance—our need to feel worthwhile, which bolsters our self-esteem. We might do this through careers, relationships, social causes, serving, and even church, to name a few. Companions of this idol often are pride and self-centeredness.

We commonly seek significance from other people—a parent, spouse, or a child, for example. Or perhaps from a boss, pastor, or best friend. Earning that person's admiration, respect, or love becomes a higher priority in our life than God. We don't feel good unless someone else is affirming our significance.

"What's your name, and what do you do?" is often one of the first things men say when they meet each other. I'm sure many women do the same. Our careers give us a feeling of significance and identity.

They're the source of our income, and that's not a bad thing, right? After all, our jobs enable us to provide for our families. We enjoy being admired by others for our leadership or accomplishments. We feel important when coworkers come to us for ideas and help. Maybe we even enjoy being with them more than with our families.

But a career can easily become a god. Ultimately, it can extract from us a whole lot more than it can ever give. Jesus and Jesus alone is our source of significance. Remember that the almighty God, your Father, makes us this promise: "For I know the plans I have for you, declares the Lord, plans for welfare and not for evil, to give you a future and a hope" (Jer. 29:11). A career will never give us a future and a hope. Only God can give us a future and a hope, and he has plans for us. The career god is a very poor substitute for God and needs to be knocked off our altar. God deserves to be there.

I'll never forget the day the Lord revealed to me that my god was not God but rather my serving God was. It was one of the most painful experiences of my life. In my heart and mind, I literally came to the point of never intending to return to a pulpit or to the ministry. In those dark and painful days, the only person I really spoke to was my wife. She will tell you I had given up and quit. I did not realize what God was doing at the time, but he was stripping away from me the god of serving him. I had to replace that god with the true God.

Other Idols

One time when Jesus was speaking about the Jewish religious leaders, who were very ritualistic, he said, " 'This people honors me with their lips, but their heart is far from me'…You have a fine way of rejecting the commandment of God in order to establish your tradition!" (Mark 7:6, 9). The Pharisees made grand spectacles of pious worship. They made sure others saw them tithing, and they stood and prayed loudly in the temple so others would see and hear them "worship." Their stubborn, proud hearts were far from being in the right place before God.

It's easy to point a finger at the Pharisees, but let's point it back at ourselves. We evangelicals may believe we are free from such temptations, but we can be the same kind of pharisaical experts today. Individuals and churches can elevate all kinds of good things of church above God.

For example, there are those who think the type of music sung during worship is of utmost importance. "If a certain type of music is played and sung, I can worship. If it's not, I can't." Some make the pastor an idol. "If such and such is preaching, I can learn and grow. If he's not, then I don't want to attend." For others it's a particular ministry or program. "I'm here at this church because of the youth ministry." For some, it's about the worship style. "I can only worship in a church that gives me the freedom to raise my hands. If I don't feel the emotion, I can't worship there." Some of us make a denomination an idol. But if you care more about your denomination and its traditions than about being a biblical church, then you've elevated it to godlike status.

Martin Luther, whom God used to bring revival to the world and to the church (and, oh, how the church needed the revival at that time!), tried "religion" as a way to make him right with God. Rather than bless him, however, all it did was leave him unsatisfied. "I kept the rule of my order so strictly that I may say that if ever a monk got to heaven by his monkery [service as a monk] it was I," Luther said. "All my brothers in the monastery who knew me will bear me out.

If I had kept on any longer, I should have killed myself with vigils, prayers, readings and other work."[9] His monkery could not get him to heaven. His position, possessions, and power couldn't. Finally, he understood that human works could not make him right with God. Only by God's grace and his work are we saved.

We must be wary of trying to earn God's approval through religious "doing." Some believe if they attend church enough, serve enough, and give enough, then they will earn God's approval (or his love). Before long, those actions have become a person's substitutes for true worship.

This application isn't limited only to the actions of attending, serving, or giving. Rituals, liturgies, or symbols can become substitutes for God. When that happens, we are worshipping religion instead of God. It isn't that we set out for that to happen. In fact, the rituals and symbols may represent an important biblical principle or character. But if they evolve to a status that replaces worship of Christ and close fellowship with him, then we've made them idols.

Please don't mistake my point; membership and commitment to a local church are vital for every healthy Christian. Nevertheless, great care must be taken to protect ourselves from worship of false gods—even at church.

We've named many types of idols, but don't forget that ideas and philosophies, governments and political parties, and diseases and disabilities all can become idols too. We can allow negative emotions such as anger, revenge, and hatred to become consuming idols. We are indeed capable of creating unlimited idols as Calvin said.

Recognizing Idols

The people and objects we turn into idols are not necessarily bad or evil. We can turn perfectly good things into idols simply by wanting them too much. "We know a good thing has become a counterfeit god when its demands on you exceed proper boundaries,"[10] according to Keller. An idol has exceeded its proper boundaries when we are willing to trust or obey the thing desired more than God—when we give it more of our time, emotions, and attention than we should, or when we want it more than we want a vibrant, growing relationship with God.

Idolatry is very self-centered and deceiving—the exact opposite of God-centered. We become very possessive of the idols we create, stubbornly clinging to them. "They're my idols and I love them," we declare by our actions.

Phidias was an ancient Greek sculptor who was particularly talented at sculpting the Greek gods. Upon completing a magnificent statue of Jupiter Olympius, he carved this on the pedestal: "Phidias, the Athenian, the Son of Charmides, Made Me."[11] My desire is that this book will help you discover what idols you've crafted and chiseled your name on.

As I said before, as human beings, we are going to worship someone or something. We are faced daily with the choice of whom or what we will make the recipient of our worship. God wants the focus of our worship to be him. He will not settle for second place in our lives. He wants us to return our idolatrous hearts to him and to the blessings and satisfaction of close fellowship with him.

I believe how he calls us to return to him can be summarized in a four-step pattern. The pastors of our church saw this pattern repeated over and over in the lives of our members. We'll take at look at the first step in the next chapter.

CHAPTER THREE

Wake-Up Call

"The Bible makes it...clear that we cannot defeat idolatry by knowledge alone. Mere intellectual dismissal of other gods is not enough. It takes a covenant love for God to root out idolatry because idolatry remains a threat even though we know with certainty that idols are nothings,"[1] says Guinness. We must have a change of heart.

But what happens if we don't discern them on our own? Or if we know we have them but choose not to turn from them? Then I believe God will intentionally and directly use some painful experiences to get our attention. In other words, he will discipline us. God wants us to stop heading in the wrong direction, so he will use the pain of discipline to wake us up to the problem.

This is the first step of his pattern to call our hearts to return to him: *God gives us a wake-up call.*

It's like a flashing red stop signal with a U-turn sign. It's that persistent voice of your GPS warning that you are going the wrong way and repeatedly urging you to "make a legal U-turn at the first opportunity." And if we ignore God's efforts to get our attention, he will step up the intensity and severity of the discipline.

I remember my first day of high school. There were hundreds of us nervous freshmen sitting in a large auditorium while the principal went through the student handbook with us. He discussed the schedule and explained what high school would be like for us because he wanted us to have a good experience. He also wanted us to know what the rules were and, when necessary, what the discipline would be to correct us and bring us back to living within those rules. If we broke a minor rule and it was the first offense, then there would be a minor consequence. He made it clear that the discipline was progressive and would escalate up to expulsion from school for the most serious infractions. I realized then and there it would be better to respond very early to the discipline.

God treats us in a similar way. We're his children. He wants to bless and protect us. He wants to encourage and use us. He gives us guidelines in the Bible for how to live a life pleasing to him. But if we stubbornly cling to our idols, rationalizing disobedience to God in order to keep them, God will use loving discipline to correct us as would any loving father with a disobedient child. His purpose is to steer us back on course to himself and his provision. He knows we can never be truly satisfied with the Christian life and can never have the abundant life he desires for us until we deal with our idolatry.

The good news is Christians can learn to discern God's discipline—hopefully before it progresses to a more painful level.

God's Discipline

"Children thrive best in an atmosphere of genuine love, undergirded by reasonable, consistent discipline....When properly applied, loving discipline works!"[2] Thousands of parents subscribe to James Dobson's advice of discipline with love. But from where do you think Dobson developed his philosophy? The Bible. Dobson always credits God's Word for his parenting guidelines. Believers are God's children; he is the parent. When we do wrong, out of love he disciplines us.

"I just love my sons too much to discipline them. I don't want to hurt them," a parent told me one time. "No, you don't love them enough because if you did, you would discipline them," I replied. And it's true. A lack of discipline does not demonstrate love. Parents will discipline their children if they truly want to see them mature, reach their full potential, and live productive lives. Our heavenly Father does likewise.

Hebrews 12:5 warns, "My son, do not regard lightly the discipline of the Lord." There are several words for the word *discipline* in the original language of the New Testament. When this verse talks about discipline, it refers to an action within a family. It's describing the efforts of parents who work to educate, train, develop, cultivate, and encourage maturity in their children.

We naturally don't like discipline. "Discipline me? Are you kidding? I'm an adult; I don't need to be disciplined." But if you are a believer, your heavenly Father will discipline you—no matter how old you are.

I remember when a man, who was in his eighties and a real spiritual giant in my estimation, told me about how God still continued to discipline him to that day. Isn't that marvelous? It's a wonderful thought that God loves us too much, regardless of how mature we are, not to discipline us.

Discipline's Two Characteristics

Biblical discipline has two primary characteristics. First, correction is always painful or restrictive. It may not be physically painful; it may be spiritually or emotionally painful.

In the first few verses of the twenty-third psalm, David beautifully uses the metaphor of his Lord as a loving shepherd. At one point he says, "your rod and your staff, they comfort me." If you were a lamb, you probably wouldn't say the shepherd's rod comforted you. David had grown up as a shepherd, so he knew sometimes a shepherd used the crook of his staff to pull a lamb back from a place of danger. But he also knew that when necessary the shepherd would strike the lamb with the rod to correct it.

If the lamb continued to stubbornly wander off from the flock after it had been disciplined, then the shepherd might actually use the rod to break one of the lamb's legs. Why? Was it because the shepherd didn't love or care for the lamb? Not at all. It was to correct the lamb for its own protection and to teach it not to wander away into trouble. In fact, the shepherd would show his care and devotion for the injured animal by carrying it on his shoulders for weeks or even months until its leg was restored completely. Through that experience, the lamb would finally learn to stay in the fold where its protection was. The fact that his heavenly Father, the Good Shepherd, loves the sheep of his flock enough to correct them comforted David.

Sometimes God's discipline is like a fence or a closed door that limits us in some way. God might say no to something we want very much because he has another plan and purpose in mind. Sometimes it's because he can foresee a destructive danger we are heading into, and he wants to stop us before we fall into serious trouble.

A very well-known biblical character was told no numerous times. One time God allowed the apostle Paul to see glimpses of heaven that other people would never see. He had experiences with God that no one else had and was given knowledge that other people were not given. Because of this, pride could present a danger for Paul. God gave him a thorn in the flesh, which Paul called a "messenger of Satan," to keep him humble.

This thorn exasperated Paul. "Three times I pleaded with the Lord about this, that it should leave me" (2 Cor. 12:8). I think he was really saying, "I keep on praying, praying, and praying 'God, stop this pain! Stop this pain! God, do something!' " Finally, Paul hears from God: "But he said to me, 'My grace is sufficient for you, for my power is made perfect in weakness' " (12:9).

Paul didn't like the pain. He didn't like the discipline—the limitation. In no way did he like the "messenger of Satan" that was sent to him, but he admitted it had driven him to the Lord and kept him from boasting. It made him realize how vulnerable and weak he was. <u>Sometimes God tells us no so we will depend on him.</u>

Secondly, correction is always done for a positive motive—to restore close fellowship with God. God introduces discipline into our lives to encourage us toward holy living, which is a life blessed and protected by him. I am not saying that a blessed life is one of material or monetary blessings. It is a blessed life because of close, fulfilling fellowship with the Lord. Although it's not easy, we must choose to look beyond the discipline, focusing on the joy of the restored relationship after the discipline.

"He disciplines us for our good, that we may share his holiness. For the moment all discipline seems painful rather than pleasant, but later it yields the peaceful fruit of righteousness" (Heb. 12:10–11). The first-century Hebrew believers were molded and shaped by the discipline they endured. They worried, struggled, and recognized that they didn't have all of the answers. As they matured, however, they moved toward a place of greater intimacy with the Lord.

They began to grow up in Christ. The painful discipline resulted in blessing.

When our sons were young, one of our favorite vacation spots was Mount Rushmore. I was fascinated by how those magnificent presidential faces had been chiseled of out of the side of a granite mountain. The man who sculpted them was Gutzon Borglum. The museum at Mount Rushmore has several articles about Gutzon and how he sculpted the faces. "Those figures were there for forty million years. All I had to do was dynamite four hundred thousand tons of granite to bring them into view,"[3] Borglum said in one article.

All he had to do was to cut away four hundred thousand tons of rock to reveal the faces! Such a simple statement for a far-from-simple task. But it is a good comparison of what God does in our lives. The divine Sculptor tries to dynamite away the unnecessary part that keeps us from looking like Jesus—those things in our lives that stand in the way of close fellowship, genuine worship, and obedient service to him. "For we are his workmanship, created in Christ Jesus for good works, which God prepared beforehand, that we should walk in them" (Eph. 2:10).

Types of God's Discipline

One of the problems many of us have is that we've never been taught to recognize God's discipline in our lives. Nor do we seem to understand how important it is to do so quickly. We're like a child sitting in her room for a time-out who has not connected the dots between what is happening to her now and her prior behavior.

Scripture provides many specific examples of God's discipline. As we look at the following methods, don't make the mistake of thinking these are the only types or that he will apply them in some cookie-cutter approach. One size does not fit all. God deals differently with each of us, so use good discernment as you consider your circumstances. For some people, his discipline might end quickly; for others, it might escalate and extend over quite a lengthy period of time.

Henry Blackaby and Claude King describe seven ways God disciplines and judges his people: "convicts of sin," "refuses to hear our prayers," "withdraws his presence," "sends a famine of his word," "removes his hedge of protection," "allows the full consequences of sin," and "destroys or removes."[4]

Although I agree with their assessment of the methods God uses to discipline us, I disagree with part of their corresponding statement: "Only after correction fails to bring change does more severe punishment and the wrath of God come."[5] My particular disagreement comes with their use of the word *punishment* in this context. I believe discipline is not punishment but rather is correction, and there is a difference. Christ took the punishment for our sins on the cross once and for all. But as believers who struggle with the sinful desires of our flesh (our ungodly, human inclinations), we will continue to venture into sin and will need to be corrected through discipline. I agree, however, with their statement that God's discipline is usually progressive.

After the stewardship banquet and as we began our more in-depth corporate study of idolatry, many members were convicted about the people and things they had allowed to be placed before God. They now realized that the symptoms they had been experiencing, such as dissatisfaction with their spiritual life or dry prayer life, were ways God was trying to get their attention through discipline. He was issuing a wake-up call.

Using Blackaby and King's basic discipline distinctions and adding a few additional ones, I've fleshed out the common ways God disciplines his children. Some are similar with only subtle differences, but putting them in separate categories helps us distinguish them. I have witnessed all of them in my years of ministry (and experienced many!) and seen more than one inflicted at a time.

It is especially frustrating to watch one of your church members experience a series of progressive disciplines, yet stubbornly refuse to turn back to God. I urge you to develop a heart that is sensitive to his discipline so you can respond quickly.

One-Way Prayer

This first type of God's discipline is characterized by one-sided conservation with God. We pray, but we see no answer. Our desires are not granted, and specific requests are never met. It would be better to see evidence of God saying no, but instead we see no evidence that God is even listening. I've had times when my prayer life would dwindle, essentially becoming ineffective because of sin.

"But your iniquities have made a separation between you and your God, and your sins have hidden his face from you so that he does not hear" (Isa. 59:2). This verse does not mean God somehow lacks knowledge of our praying. Instead, it means he does not listen to, respond to, or answer.

Does it seem like God is not answering your prayers as he has in the past? Do you feel like your prayers are going no farther than the ceiling and then falling lamely to the floor? Is prayer becoming increasingly difficult for you? Do you sense that your prayer life is very much off track? Are you praying less and less? If you're answering yes to these questions, God may be choosing not to respond to you.

When we don't see God answering our prayers, or if our prayer life has flat-lined, it may well be God is trying to give us a wake-up call.

Silence

Though similar to "one-way prayer," silence used as discipline is more specifically related to not hearing God speak through his Word. We may go through periods of reading the Bible and receiving nothing from it. It's only words, sentences, paragraphs, and pages. We aren't given insight into what the Lord is saying. We don't see how it applies to us. We may gain information but not the kind of wisdom that changes our lives. God's communication through his Word seems to have dried up like a small pond during a summer drought. Once we enjoyed reading the Bible and it seemed alive to us. Now under this discipline, the pages remain silent.

Abandoned

Sometimes God will discipline us by leaving us alone. He seems to vacate our souls. This does not mean he has totally abandoned us. But it does mean he may not manifest himself to us in the clear ways he had before.

For example, the warmth and fire of our "first love" experience with the Lord has grown cold, distant, and dry. Our relationship with him has become merely academic, liturgical, or ritualistic. Our intimacy and joy in the Lord has diminished and church has become laborious and unfulfilling. When we listen to sermons, we don't discern any new spiritual insights. The peace of a fulfilling relationship with God has been replaced with an unsettling sense of dissatisfaction. Any real experience with God is just a distant memory. Our enemy, Satan, seems to have the upper hand in our lives. Unfortunately, he also uses this as an opportunity to plant doubts about our salvation, question our worth to God, or create feelings of hopelessness.

Saul, the first king of Israel, experienced God's abandonment after his repeated disobedience. "Saul was afraid of David because the Lord was with him but had departed from Saul" (1 Sam. 18:12). Saul knew the power and authority of the Lord that once rested on him were now gone, given to another.

Aaron and Miriam are another example. They complained about Moses, ostensibly because he married a Cushite woman but more obviously because they were jealous that he enjoyed such special favor with the Lord. First, the Lord leveled a stinging chastisement against them, and then he departed (Num. 12:9–11).

Loss of intimacy with God ought to break our hearts and turn us back to Him.

Loss of Influence

God may also discipline us by extinguishing our "light." At the beginning of Revelation, Jesus tells John to pen specific messages to the seven churches located in Asia Minor. Although our Lord had a lot of good to say to the church in Ephesus, he also criticized them (and us today): "Remember therefore from where you have fallen; repent, and do the works you did at first. If not, I will come to you and remove your lampstand from its place, unless you repent" (2:5).

The "lampstand" refers to our influence, or our witness and usefulness. If it were removed, we would no longer have a voice in spiritual leadership. Rather than people being drawn by the Spirit to learn from us and see Jesus in us, they would simply quit listening.

He would stop giving us opportunities to witness. God's redemptive work around us would become rare and limited in scope. It's a warning applicable to both individuals and churches.

Bible and theology professor Wayne Grudem offers this insight about our diminished effectiveness:

> When we sin as Christians, it is not only our personal relationship with God that is disrupted. Our Christian life and fruitfulness in ministry are also damaged. Jesus warns us, "As the branch cannot bear fruit by itself, unless it abides in the vine, neither can you, unless you abide in me" (John 15:4). When we stray from fellowship with Christ because of sin in our lives, we diminish the degree to which we are abiding in Christ....We will inevitably feel some loss of spiritual strength, some diminution of spiritual power, some loss of effectiveness in the work of God's kingdom.[6]

The Ephesian church practiced proper doctrine and was actively committed to serving the Lord. It had a long history and was the most prominent church in the area,[7] and yet Jesus had this complaint about the Ephesian Christians: they had abandoned their first love. They had replaced their deep devotion for the Lord with some secondary fascination. By now, we should know exactly what this is called: idolatry. Jesus implored the Ephesians to remember their first love.

Ephesus was a city full of idol worship. In fact, it was known as "temple keeper of the great Artemis" (Acts 19:35), a pagan goddess. Acts also tells us how the local idol makers were upset with Paul's preaching. It was bad for business because when people turned to Jesus, they quit buying idols.

Maybe the Ephesian Christians started to become tolerant of idol worship, no longer wanting to offend those who chose to participate in pagan worship or made a living crafting idols. Or maybe some of them were tempted to follow the doctrines of the Nicolaitans, even though John compliments them for hating the Nicolaitans (Rev. 2:6). They probably didn't purposely leave their first love, but by not guarding against it, gradually it happened.

That is what happens when we know we are neglecting our relationship with the Lord but continue to do it anyway. God's wake-up call is a call to remember from where we have fallen—to remember what it was like when he had first place in our hearts and we had a vibrant relationship with him.

Remember how our students framed the Silver Cliff Covenant and hung it in a prominent place? They realized the importance of not forgetting what God had done in their lives, and they understood that the week was too significant to become "just another summer camp experience." Remembering those times when we are especially close to him can be an effective motivator to keep our hearts free of idols and right with God.

Reduced Circle of Protection

"And now I will tell you what I will do to my vineyard [his people]. I will remove its hedge, and it shall be devoured; I will break down its wall, and it shall be trampled down" (Isa. 5:5). God warned Isaiah that his protection surrounding the Israelites was going to be lifted for a while. It was a drastic measure of discipline. Whereas the previously mentioned discipline category "abandoned" is more of an inner, spiritual abandonment, this example of discipline is more of a physical, environmental one.

Understand God will not totally remove his defense and protection. We could not survive if he did. But if we continue long enough in rebellion against him, usually we will experience progressively greater consequences of our sin, which means experiencing more intense suffering as God pulls back his protective care.

I have witnessed this increasing discipline in people's lives. As a person plunges deeper and deeper into sin, moving farther and farther away from God, the level of God's protection is reduced. The person may experience a convergence of many bad things happening all at once, leaving him or her feeling overwhelmed and without hope.

I remember receiving a telephone call many years ago from a young man named Scott, who was a member of a church I once pastored. He had committed himself to full-time ministry and was in his senior year in college. After graduation, he planned to attend seminary. When I answered the phone, he barely got out my name and began to cry. I recognized his voice, so I asked him what was wrong.

He proceeded to tell me how his world was falling apart. His girlfriend had left him. His work in a small church as a youth director had gone from good to bad overnight. He had lost his wallet and with it his identification and money. School was going so poorly he didn't know if he was going to graduate, and his parents were so angry at him that they wouldn't talk to him. "Why is God doing this to me?" he asked.

I tried to lift his mood by joking with him for a minute about why these things were happening. But then I turned serious and asked him to tell me about his walk with Jesus. After a long pause, he admitted that his relationship with Jesus now was a mere shadow of what it used to be. "Is there sin in your life God has convicted you of but you've rationalized and justified it, and you're living in it?" I asked. When he confessed that there was, I gently reminded him that perhaps God had removed his protection so that he would see how desperately he needed him.

A week later, there was a message from Scott. Before I had the chance to call him back, he called me again that evening. "Dennis, God has restored me to himself," he said. We cried together in joy and thankfulness. For this young man, it took a reduction of God's protection to turn his attention back to him.

Reduced protection could be manifested in many ways: sickness or other kinds of physical or emotional ailments; limited opportunities; a business failure; or relationship difficulties. In essence, life becomes much tougher because of the circumstances happening to us.

Discipline by the Church

God might also choose to use the local church as his instrument of discipline. Unfortunately, many churches have abandoned this God-given responsibility. It may be because pastors are afraid to administer it. Some are ignorant of the subject; others have an incomplete understanding of the church's responsibilities.

Pastors and members alike often believe kindness, patience, and tolerance are the only guiding principles for a church's relationship with its members. That mistaken belief, however, ignores the undeniable teaching of Scripture that the church is also required to have a saved and holy fellowship—and to do what it takes to maintain it.[8] Clearly the Lord uses the intervention of brothers and sisters in Christ to gain a sinning Christian's attention. In certain circumstances, the kindest act a church can do for a member is to lovingly point out a sin and encourage repentance.

Idol Removal

If we stubbornly ignore God's previous efforts to discipline us, he may progress to removal of our idol. He may move us away from jobs or people. He may remove wealth or demote us to a position of lesser prestige. He may end jobs or relationships—whatever it takes for you to give up your idol.

With great regret, one woman admitted to me how she had created a god out of her position at work. At one time she had been a devoted church member, taught a Bible study for children, and was a good wife and mother. Then she took a sales position and started making a lot of money. With her financial rewards came trips, titles, and recognition. But time demands and pressures began to extract a toll. The first thing she stepped away from was ministry; then she became unfaithful in church attendance. As sin begins to strengthen its grip on a person, ministry and church activities are always the first things to be abandoned. It's a pattern I've observed countless times.

Finally, her relationship with her husband and children deteriorated. Literally, within eighteen months, all she had left was her new god. She had traded her family and the joy of her relationship with Christ and the church for a god that only left her empty. Eventually, God removed her idol.

The Ultimate Discipline

This last type of discipline is by far the most severe. "If anyone sees his brother committing a sin not leading to death, he shall ask, and God will give him life—to those who commit sins that do not lead to death. There is sin that leads to death; I do not say that one should pray for that. All wrongdoing is sin, but there is sin that does not lead to death" (1 John 5:16–17). Notice the word *a* in the first line of the verse. English translators have added it to try to make the passage read more smoothly for us, but it would have been better if they hadn't because it changes the meaning. The Greek manuscript of the passage does not say "a sin" but rather "sin." The passage is not trying to say there is one specific sin that leads to death, but rather a category of sin that leads to death.

John first tells us there is sin that does not lead to death, and God corrects that kind of sin. Then he tells us that there is sin that leads to death. This kind of sin is when we continue to ignore the discipline of God, where even though we are saved we continue to live like a lost person. Some call it "continued carnality." The present tense verb for *commit* here means "sinning as a lifestyle, as a way of life."

God can, as an ultimate act of discipline, take us out of the world because we reject his call back to him. The Bible shows us at least two instances of this.

Ananias and Sapphira deceitfully misled fellow believers in order to impress others with how charitable and religious they were (Acts 5:1–11). Maybe this had been a pattern in their lives, and this time God chose not to tolerate their hypocritical actions any longer. To make sure their deceitful hearts didn't pollute others in the church, he struck them dead. He simply took them out of the world.

In another instance, some people continued to take the Lord's Supper in an unworthy manner and had been unwilling to judge themselves (1 Cor. 11:27–30). The result was that some of the group became weak and sick; some died.

Many years ago I was acquainted with a woman who had continued in carnality and a destructive lifestyle for years. God tried to get her attention through various types of discipline, which she stubbornly ignored. Finally and unexpectedly at a very young age, I am absolutely positive God at last said, "I've had enough. Your life is useless to me on the earth. I'm just going to take you on home." I believe her death was the result of God's ultimate discipline. I am not saying everyone who dies at an early age dies under God's discipline. But I am telling you God's Word says it can happen and it does. It's a sobering thought.

As difficult as these things are to read, they are equally difficult to write. But no father who loves his children would refuse to discipline them or refuse to tell them how he will discipline them if the need arises. In his Word, God does just that. He explains how he will discipline us so that we can learn to discern the discipline and identify our actions that led to it.

Isaiah's Crisis

The prophet Isaiah's life offers a specific example of God's wake-up call. A young Isaiah begins telling us a story about an incredible heavenly scene. First, he identifies the year as he writes, "In the year that King Uzziah died I saw the Lord sitting upon a throne" (Isa. 6:1). Why is when the vision happened such an important fact? First of all, it was a very significant event in his life, so Isaiah is simply marking the date of his heavenly vision by it.

We do the same thing, don't we? For those of us who live in the Oklahoma City area as I do, we might say, "I remember it was the year the Murrah Federal Building was bombed." Many of us would do the same thing with 9/11. It's common to associate a significant event with some other significant event, and in this case, Isaiah associates his vision with the year King Uzziah died.

Secondly, I think King Uzziah was very important to Isaiah. I suspect he idolized him, and his death was Isaiah's painful wake-up call. If God had not taken Uzziah off Isaiah's throne, he may have never seen God sitting on the heavenly throne. The idol standing in the way had to be removed first.

Let's review the setting of Isaiah's story. The year? Either 740 or 739 BC. The place? Jerusalem, the capital city of the Southern Kingdom called Judah. The event? The crisis created by the death of King Uzziah.

Uzziah (also called Azariah) ascended to the throne after his father Amaziah died. You might think that's a lot of "-iahs" and let's just move on to the interesting part, but take a minute to understand why God included this information for us.

Amaziah was known for establishing a great army for Judah. Before his reign, the country only had a small militia. But under Amaziah's leadership, Judah had built up a great army. Whereas the Bible tells us Amaziah did right in the eyes of the Lord, it also adds this caveat: "yet not with a whole heart" (2 Chron. 25:2), which was unmistakably demonstrated by his grievous mistakes. He never did remove the high places of idol worship that his father allowed. Furthermore, after a great victory over the Edomites, their arch-enemy, Amaziah took some of the pagan idols of Edom, brought them back to Jerusalem, worshipped them, and made offerings to them.

Why he would want to worship the gods of the people he had just defeated, which would obviously mean they were not very powerful gods, is a question that can only be answered by the fact that God didn't have his whole heart. As his relationship with God grew distant, other substitutes, even powerless ones, grew more alluring.

God began to discipline Amaziah and removed his blessings. Soon the army of Judah was defeated and Jerusalem was repeatedly sacked by their enemies. As expected, the people of Judah blamed Amaziah for what had happened. Eventually, they assassinated him.

His son Uzziah ascended to the throne of Judah at only sixteen years of age. Can you imagine becoming king of a nation at that age? He was a good king during his fifty-two-year reign, and he left a legacy of good projects. For example, he led the people to strengthen the walls around Jerusalem. The result was that hordes of marauding invaders were turned away, and Jerusalem was no longer constantly defeated by enemies. In addition, Uzziah was a promoter of agriculture. He rebuilt the nation's agricultural system so that the people wouldn't suffer severe famine. Most importantly, though, he decided to reject the gods of the Edomites, which his father had established in Judah. He pledged to have no gods but God.

Uzziah was not perfect. His pride led him to make some severe and destructive mistakes toward the end of his life, but he did lead Judah to undeniable prosperity and great success. No doubt he was a very popular king among the people of Judah.

This background information helps us understand how devastated they must have felt when their beloved king suddenly died. The closest America has ever come to a similar emotional experience with a president may have been near the end of World War II when President Franklin Roosevelt died. He had led our country through the tumultuous time of war, and his death created an emotional upheaval for our countrymen.

Isaiah and the people of Judah had become dependent on

Uzziah. He had become their security and hope. But God will not tolerate his people turning to another god without desperately trying to get their attention. I'm not saying idolatry is the only reason God disciplines believers, but it is a big one. The king's death was a painful wake-up call.

Is All Adversity Discipline?

I can't close this chapter without addressing the question, is all adversity God's discipline? The short answer? No. The fact is, good Christians who love Jesus experience trials and pain, and the reasons are varied. Sometimes it's because of God's discipline, as we've just outlined. Other times it's not.

I don't listen to television preachers very often. It isn't that I have anything against them as a group, but television does have its way of attracting the outer limits of the preaching ministry. While channel surfing one time, I came across a very excited preacher. "If you really love Jesus and if you really have faith, then you'll have no pain in your life, you'll never get sick, and you'll have lots of money, health, and prosperity. If you really love Jesus, you're just not going to have any problems. Just love Jesus, and everything will be perfect from now on," he was essentially telling his audience.

It reminded me of that old hymn:
Every day with Jesus is sweeter than the day before.
Every day with Jesus, I love Him more and more;
Jesus saves and keeps me, and He's the One I'm waiting for.
Every day with Jesus is sweeter than the day before.[9]

There's only one thing wrong with that theology. You can't find it in the Bible.

It's tragic that some churches erroneously promote "health and prosperity" as a biblical teaching. "God wants you to be wealthy so that you can enjoy the fine things money can buy. God wants you to enjoy the pleasures of good health," they tell people.

That philosophy can even take root in and develop in Christians, who until that time have been quite sincere in their faith, lived for the Lord, and wanted to honor the Lord. Regrettably, when these Christians experience some loss, pain, or difficulty, which will eventually happen, they will accuse God of betraying them. They will act as if they're owed only the good things in life from him.

Sometimes we face great times of temptations and struggles because, unfortunately, we have an enemy that is very powerful. God's Word says we struggle against the spiritual forces of this world (Eph. 6:12) and that "the devil prowls around like a roaring lion, seeking someone to devour" (1 Pet. 5:8). How does the devil devour us? By devouring the time we have set aside for God but instead spend it on other distractions. By devouring the spirit to serve others and tell them about Jesus, convincing us we're not able to do so. By attacking our loved ones and trying to cultivate attitudes of hate, distrust, and consuming despair in us. By tempting us with all kinds of pleasurable, good things that become idols.

One time I received a call from a woman whose husband had told her he wanted a divorce. She began to tell me about the months and months of fighting that had been going on between them. Interestingly, she said she had come to understand something about this difficult time: it wasn't her husband who was causing this. She believed it was Satan who was doing this to them, and she was right.

You may think your boss is out to destroy you. No, Satan is

out to destroy you. You may think that no-good neighbor of yours wants to drive you crazy. No, it is Satan who wants to drive you crazy. You may think that teacher in school has it out for you and wants you to suffer. No, it is Satan who has it out for you. There are evil forces in this world—Satan and his demons—that want to destroy your life.

Of course, God also gives us trials to teach us lessons such as dependence and perseverance.

Although a season of pain in our lives is easily recognizable, what is much more complicated is how to discern the nature of a painful event. In other words, how can we discern if this trial is a natural consequence of living in a fallen world, if it's an expression of God's discipline related to unconfessed sin, or if God has allowed it for another purpose?

While the issue is perplexing, it need not be problematic for sincere Christians. Whether a season of suffering is due to the consequences of the world's corruption or is more directly prescribed by the hand of God, the results should be the same: the pain and trials of our lives should remind us of our weakness and God's power.

What If You Don't Experience Discipline?

What if you think God has never disciplined you before? It could be for one of two reasons.

First, you might not recognize the hand of God in the pain you are experiencing. You may have never been taught that God disciplines his children and haven't considered that the adversities, limitations, and painful situations you've gone through in your life may have been there for the purpose of discipline. As I mentioned before, this is a common problem among Christians. I challenge pastors and church leaders to do a better job at teaching their congregations about God's discipline.

The second reason may well be because you are an "illegitimate child." "If [in this instance, *if* means "if, and some of you are"] you are left without discipline, in which all have participated, then you are illegitimate children and not sons" (Heb. 12:8). Why were there some people in the church who were not being disciplined by God? Because they did not belong to him in the first place. They weren't his children; they were illegitimate children who were "sitting in" with God's kids. He punishes illegitimate children at times, but he does not discipline them. Discipline is intended to turn hearts *back* to God—where they previously were.

If you are not sure you are a Christian and want to have a personal relationship with Jesus Christ, I urge you to do so now. See the appendix for more information about receiving God's free gift of salvation.

Tragically, even after God's numerous attempts to turn their hearts back to him through discipline, many Christians continue to ignore him, choosing to selfishly serve their own idols instead. They end up settling for worldly desires that never fully satisfy instead of enjoying a vibrant, fulfilling experience with the Lord.

Don't harden your heart toward God when discipline comes into your life. Seek the Lord. Be willing to open your spirit to what he wants to reveal to you: himself.

CHAPTER FOUR

Revelation

How do you picture God? A kindly, old man with white hair sitting in a rocking chair, smiling and nodding approvingly at you? A tyrannical father who keeps you under his thumb, waiting for you to mess up so he can punish you? Or maybe like a heavenly butler or genie, to be summoned only when you need something? Perhaps a good luck charm? "Can't hurt to have God on my side." Let me tell you. We won't find these descriptions of God in the Bible.

The great Christians in history did not understand God to be a gentle grandpa, dictator, or genie. Instead, when they broke away from their self-centeredness, self-indulgence, and self-worship, God revealed himself in powerful ways. Then they began to view and pursue God as he actually is—not as what they wanted him to be or for what they wanted from him.

I find it perplexing that so many Christians today seem to have forgotten who God really is. There is no way they could treat him the way they do if they truly believed him for what he is and who he is. They have lost awe and respect for the almighty Creator, allowing almost too much casualness and familiarity in their understanding of him. I believe many evangelicals are guilty of this.

Others have effectively ignored God's revelation of himself through Scripture. Instead, they have allowed today's popular pseudo-Christian books to influence them, regardless of how unbiblically they may depict God. They have been easily convinced that these authors' smooth, persuasive, albeit incorrect, arguments with their skewed theology are messages of truth.

Christians today need a fresh, accurate vision of the awesome purity and the complete holiness of God. That's what I believe will happen for those who heed God's wake-up call. The Bible says when God's people remember who he is and turn their hearts and minds to him, then God will reveal himself for all that he truly is.

This is the second step of calling idolaters back to him: *God will reveal himself to us.*

When he does, we will get a renewed vision and understanding of the pure and holy God. Be prepared though, because at the same time we'll painfully see our sin more clearly than ever before as it is contrasted to his holiness. This chapter deals with those two issues: God's holiness and our sin. It's a chapter of opposites but also of hope.

Isaiah's Heavenly Vision

After Isaiah's wake-up call, God revealed himself in a magnificent revelation.

> In the year that King Uzziah died I saw the Lord sitting upon a throne, high and lifted up; and the train of his robe filled the temple. Above him stood the seraphim. Each had six wings: with two he covered his face, and with two he covered his feet, and with two he flew. And one called to another and said: "Holy, holy, holy is the Lord of hosts; the whole earth is full of his glory!" And the foundations of the thresholds shook at the voice of

him who called, and the house was filled with smoke (Isa. 6:1–4).

What an incredible vision into the very throne room of heaven. God allowed Isaiah an encounter with him like none other. Don't hurry through this passage. Read it several times. Meditate on it. Close your eyes and try to imagine it. Listen for the sound of the rhythmic motion of the angels' wings and their melodic voices chanting "holy, holy, holy." Picture the blinding brightness emanating from God's presence and filling the entire temple. Feel his voice as it thunders through the throne room. There can't possibly be human words to adequately describe the heavenly scene Isaiah witnessed, nor how he must have felt standing in the presence of God. God's complete holiness and purity captivated him.

The Bible says no man has seen God and lived, meaning that no one has ever seen God in *all* of his glory and his splendor and lived. But there have been times when men have been privileged to see a self-revealed glimpse of God. This is one of those times. During the Old Testament era in which the book of Isaiah was written, the self-revealed glory of God, known as the *Shekinah* glory of God, was visibly recognized and sometimes referred to as smoke. That is what is being spoken of here. The *Shekinah* glory of the presence of God filled the temple.

The number three is the number of perfection in the Bible. The fact that the angels are chanting a triad of holies to describe God symbolizes that he is completely and perfectly holy. These magnificent, heavenly, sinless beings could do nothing but worship in the presence of the perfect purity and the absolute holiness of God. They are totally enthralled with his holiness.

Furthermore, their posture demonstrates worship and humility.

These six-winged angels covered their faces with two wings so as not to look directly at God's glory, covered their feet with two wings in a gesture of humble service, and flew with two wings.

A simple definition of the word *holy* is "set apart." God's holiness is everything that makes him unlike us. With regard to his character, he is perfect and without blemish. His holiness is the one character trait that touches everything he does. With regard to sin, he existed before sin and has never taken part in any sin. His purity? Crystalline. It has never been marred, nor has it been adulterated. We are totally inadequate to describe and understand the absolute, complete, perfect holiness of God.

When God reveals himself to us in a fresh way, we see clearly that God is holy, and we are not. God is pure; we are not. God is sinless; we are not. Our sin is magnified infinitely compared to God's revealed holiness.

The Essence of Sin

The majority of Americans consider sin archaic—an old-fashioned, laughable concept. Excluding the times you hear it talked about in church or in some other Christian setting, when was the last time you heard someone talk about sin? It has become a forgotten word in our society.

Sin began to disappear from the American vocabulary as our culture became more and more permeated with a philosophy called secular humanism. This philosophy has greatly influenced today's moral attitudes and values. It is a religion in itself and a prime example of idolatry. Humanism's basic belief is that man himself is the measure for everything that happens, which is a stark contradiction to the biblical principle that God and God alone sets the standards—that God and God alone states what is right and what is wrong. We live in a society in which the primary god is not God; it is ourselves.

Secularism is an age-old problem. Schlossberg says, "Eve was the first humanist....The serpent tempted her with a religious argument. She could be like God, having knowledge and power. She could be wise apart from God. The physical attraction of the fruit clearly was intended to be ancillary. What was to be fed was her pride, and what would grow was her appetite for self-worship."[1]

Just as Eve did, we are a generation practicing *inward-focused* worship rather than *God-focused* worship. "Modernity's replacement of 'top down' God-centered living with 'bottom up' human-centered living represents a titanic revolution in human history and experience,"[2] says Guinness of our society. Although philosophers may smugly point out that our society has moved beyond modernism and on to post-modernism, his assessment is still very current.

Some of us have a rather casual understanding of sin, and we don't grasp the seriousness of it. We might pray, "Oh, God, forgive me of my sins" once a month and then go merrily on our way, thinking we've done our "christianly" duty with regard to sin. But we cannot afford to be flippant about it. Sin is serious, and we must come to understand how deceptive and destructive it is.

Theologians have attempted to determine the essential nature of sin through examination of idolatry, selfishness, pride, sensuality, rebellion, unbelief, and disruption of *shalom* (the Hebrew word for peace, contentment, satisfaction). Theological professor R. Stanton Norman responds to those efforts with this assessment:

In light of the shortcomings of the other perspectives,

idolatry is the best option for our understanding of the core essence of sin. The displacement of God can be regarded as the cause for all the other manifestations of sin. Rebellion, sensuality, selfishness, unbelief, and the disruption of shalom are the results of our sinful attempts to displace God. The notion that idolatry is the essence of all sin is further strengthened by the fact that the first commandment given by God in the Ten Commandments was that "you shall have no other gods before me" (Ex. 20:3). This commandment reveals the absolute importance God places upon our exclusive worship of Him. Jesus reiterated the magnitude of this command when he said, "Love the Lord your God with all your heart, and with all your soul, and with all your mind. This is the greatest and first commandment" (Matt. 22:37–38). Idolatry is the antithesis to this commandment.[3]

The essence of sin? Idolatry.

According to God's standard, it is very clear. When we let our hearts wander away from God to idols, we are engaging in idolatry, which bluntly stated is sin. If we have any doubts about that, or of God's intolerance of sin, consider just two of numerous verses in the Bible describing the sin of idolatry.

"But you shall devote them to complete destruction, the Hittites and the Amorites, the Canaanites and the Perizzites, the Hivites and the Jebusites, as the Lord your God has commanded, that they may not teach you to do according to all their abominable practices that they have done for their gods, and so you sin against the Lord your God" (Deut. 20:17–18). How does this verse describe idolatry? Abominable. Another version says detestable.

"The next day Moses said to the people, 'You have sinned a great sin. And now I will go up to the Lord; perhaps I can make atonement for your sin.' So Moses returned to the Lord and said, 'Alas, this people has sinned a great sin. They have made for themselves gods of gold' " (Ex. 32:30–31). Idolatry was not only sin; it was great sin.

Hamartia—Stepping Away

In the Bible there are eight Greek and Hebrew words for sin that are translated into the one English word. The basic word for it in the New Testament is *hamartia*. In fact, it is used one hundred and seventy-three times. I'd say God is letting us know it is a subject requiring a great deal of attention. *Hamartia* means "to miss the mark, to err, to be mistaken, to wander from the path, and to do wrong."

The phrase *stepping away* is a good analogy of what it is like when we sin. Each time we sin, we wander farther from the path God has laid before us. Step by step we move farther away from the intimacy, protection, provision, and blessing of God.

"Thus says the Lord: 'What wrong did your fathers find in me that they went far from me, and went after worthlessness, and became worthless?' " (Jer. 2:5). It's as if God is asking, "Did your fathers see something in me that was so hideous and repulsive that when they saw it they just turned and started walking away from me, participating in one sinful activity after another? Didn't they understand that they were walking away into worthlessness, becoming more worthless the farther they got from me?"

That is what sin is—choosing to walk away from God. It's like the plaque in my office that says, "God didn't leave me, I've left him." God may abandon us for a while during times of discipline, but the more likely situation is that we abandon God. Isaiah gives us this unflattering description of the rebellious Israelites: "Ah, sinful nation, a people laden with iniquity, offspring of evildoers, children who deal corruptly! They have forsaken [abandoned] the Lord, they have despised the Holy One of Israel, they are utterly estranged" (Isa. 1:4).

Don't we do the same thing? We take one step after the next, and when we finally stop and look up, we realize we're far away from God and standing in the middle of sin. We have abandoned our close fellowship with the Lord.

Let me be clear. If you're a Christian, I don't mean you can walk away from your salvation. You can, however, walk away from the intimacy, joy, and power of your relationship with God. It is a slow, gradual process, but each time you put other things before God, you add more distance between you and him. Sadly, there are Christians who settle for this distant fellowship for weeks, months, or even years.

Characteristics of Sin

The *modus operandi* of sin is deception. For example, did Satan tell Eve what would really happen if she ate the fruit? Of course not! He deceived her. He is *the* master of deception and "deceiver of the whole world" (Rev. 12:9). If we could understand and apply this truth in our daily lives, it would change our view of sin. "Take care lest your heart be deceived, and you turn aside and serve other gods and worship them" (Deut. 11:16). And Hebrews cautions us not to "be hardened by the deceitfulness of sin" (3:13).

At first glance, sin might appear beautiful and appealing, but in reality it is a filthy, dirty thing. James uses the word *filthiness* to describe sin (James 1:21). He speaks of it as moral filthiness and compares what we should be doing with it to that of removing filthy clothes.

It makes me think of the television show "Dirty Jobs," which is about people who do jobs so dirty and disgusting that most people would never think of doing them. Those people have got to want to remove their dirty, stinking clothing just as quickly as they can when the job is done. There's no way they would keep on their filthy work clothes when they sit down at the dinner table with their family or friends when they go home. And yet, that is what we try to do—come to the table of fellowship with God, still clothed in the filthiness of idolatry.

Sin's Consequences

Most of us either venture into sin without thinking about the consequences or we deceive ourselves into thinking there won't be any. "Do not be deceived: God is not mocked, for whatever one sows, that will he also reap" (Gal. 6:7). That verse sums up the "Law of the Harvest," which involves three basic principles: (1) you reap what you sow, (2) you reap later than you sow, and (3) you reap more than you sow. We may desperately wish it weren't so, but God may allow us to reap just enough of what we have been doing to turn our hearts back to him. If we continue in rebellious sin, however, he will allow us to reap the full consequences.

I'll never forget the time a girl in her late teens came to my office, sat down, and said, "I'm pregnant. How could God have done this?"

I told her I did not believe this was a case of immaculate conception and tried to gently point out that she was reaping what she had sown. We shouldn't blame God for the consequences of our actions because we are simply reaping what we have sown.

Have you witnessed the suffering that is created in people's lives because of the consequences of sin, or felt it in your own life? Holiness does not create such suffering. Sometimes there is pain associated with holiness, but there is never torment and distress associated with it. Anguish of body, soul, and spirit comes from sin. In turn, that suffering is passed on to the people who love you the most.

Some of the most popular radio and television preachers of our society have been degraded because of sin in their lives. These men who once stood for the Lord and had positions of influence stumbled because they followed their lust for worldly pleasures. We may not experience the very public degradation they have, yet each of us experiences it to some extent when we sin. Every single sin degrades us, staining and defeating us as followers of Christ. No one is immune to sin's degradation. It degrades us in God's sight, it degrades us in the sight of others, and it degrades us in our own sight.

Never forget that sin promises one thing and delivers another. It promises success, but it never delivers godly success. It promises pleasure, but it often results in guilt. It promises happiness, but it can never provide soul-satisfying joy. Our idols promise us fulfillment and contentment with life through love, significance, security and pleasure, but they will always disappoint us eventually. Idols are temporary and will topple. Only God can give us lasting peace and a satisfying life as we grow to depend on him and his provision.

Sin is not nearly as beautiful as what we tend to think it is and Satan wants us to believe it is. It is deception to believe stepping away from God and taking part in something that filthy and degrading will somehow make us happier in life. God wants us to see sin for what it really is—something hideous standing in the way of our relationship with the pure, holy, and righteous God.

Sin Is Disobedience

Grudem offers this straightforward definition of sin: "Sin is any failure to conform to the moral law of God in act, attitude, or nature."[4] In other words, when we disobey God we sin. Sin is rebellion against our Creator. It strikes at the very being of God and defies him.

In Leviticus 26:27 God calls the Israelites' disobedience walking "contrary" to him, which means "opposite." Do we see our idolatry as doing the exact opposite of what God desires? If we are contrary to what God wants, it means we're unwilling to submit to him in obedience. If we would come to understand sin in those terms, we would be much less likely to sin and more willing to submit to his authority.

Saul the first king of Israel, struggled with obedience. He began his reign as a godly man and was a great and mighty warrior. At one point, God ordered Saul to attack Israel's enemy, the Amalekites. Saul and his army would be God's tool to disperse retribution for the years of terror these brutal descendants of Esau had inflicted on them. God's battle plan? Utterly destroy all the Amalekites and everything they own. So Saul obediently led his army into battle, and predictably, God gave them victory over the murderous Amalekites (1 Sam. 15).

The problem came after the battle. Plan A, God's plan, wasn't good enough, so Saul created Plan B, his plan. When Saul laid eyes on the great number of sheep and cattle of the defeated Amalekites, he decided the better idea was to keep them instead of destroying them.

When confronted with his disobedience, Saul argued that he actually had obeyed God. He shifted the blame to the people, saying they were the ones who wanted to keep the animals because they wanted to use them later for sacrifices to God.

We don't know if that's what he or the people really intended, but one thing is certain. Ultimately, Saul was responsible for not destroying the Amalekites' livestock, and not doing so was blatant disobedience to God's instructions. Furthermore, he didn't kill all the Amalekites as he was commanded. He kept their king alive as a prisoner.

Why did Saul disobey God? I think he selfishly sought to bolster his popularity among the people of Israel by showing off the spoils of his victory and parading the Amalekite king as a slave. I think he wanted to increase his personal wealth, and I think he let his desires for significance, popularity, security, and wealth become his gods. He was guilty of rebellion, arrogance, disobedience, and yes, idolatry against God.

God didn't ignore his disobedience. Through the prophet Samuel, God asked Saul, "Has the Lord as great delight in burnt offerings and sacrifices, as in obeying the voice of the Lord?" (1 Sam. 15:22). His question penetrated straight to the heart of the issue. After the victory, Saul kept the animals, ostensibly to sacrifice them to God. Whether he ever offered the animals as sacrifices or intended to is debatable, but clearly the question was, does God want sacrifices or obedience? "Behold, to obey is better than sacrifice" (v. 22). This applies to us today too. Obeying what God says to do and giving him first place in our hearts is what God wants of us.

In another passage about obedience, the Lord says, "But this command I gave them: 'Obey my voice, and I will be your God, and you shall be my people. And walk in all the way that I command you, that it may be well with you.' But they did not obey or incline their ear, but walked in their own counsels and the stubbornness of their evil hearts, and went backward and not forward." (Jer. 7:23–24).

The Christian life is a process of maturing to know God more intimately and understand how he wants us to live our lives. The process is called *sanctification*. The better we grow to know him, the greater heart we will have for not sinning. Ideally, this maturation process is a continuum of forward progress for Christians.

But look at the progress of the people in this passage. Jeremiah rebuked them for their disobedience, following the "counsel" of their own minds. In other words, they made their own decisions about what they would do. Their evil hearts led them to rebel against God, and they *went backward and not forward.*

Sadly, it is possible to regress in our relationship with the Lord. Christians can grow in maturity and experience dynamic intimacy with God, but if ("when" is the better word because we will) we begin to disobey him, we will quickly regress.

Jesus said, "If you love Me, you will keep my commandments" (John 14:15). Isn't that striking? He says we can tell the depth of our intimacy with him and the fervency of our love for him by the way we obey his commandments. We cannot say we love Jesus and not keep his commandments. A few verses later Jesus elaborates, "Whoever has my commandments and keeps them, he it is who loves me. And he who loves me will be loved by my Father, and I will love him and manifest myself to him" (v. 21).

Obedience holds the promise of personal fellowship with the Lord: "Come now, let us reason together, says the Lord: though your sins are like scarlet, they shall be as white as snow; though they are red like crimson, they shall become like wool. If you are willing and obedient, you shall eat the good of the land; but if you refuse and rebel, you shall be eaten by the sword" (Isa. 1:18–20).

Do you hear the words of relationship? The great promise of obedience results in being able to "eat the good of the land," which refers to having the very best life possible. It is a blessed life of intimate fellowship with God.

Some people see obedience to God as a restriction, a chain around their necks, or as a prison confining them. It is not shackles; it is not prison. It is the best life. Yet time and time again Christians find themselves drawn into sin, choosing to disregard the instructions God has given us in his Word.

It may be that God has revealed what he wants us to do, but our response has been to say, "No. I'm not going to do it. I'm going to go my own way. I'm going to do my own thing." Just like Eve, Saul, and countless others, we think we have a better plan. We don't think God's way is best for us. We want to live *our* lives *our* way. A heart filled with stubborn disobedience will result in the tragic inability to hear what God is saying to us.

Nothing is more important than learning to obey the Lord, and doing whatever it is he asks of you. Give up your idols, take yourself and your desires off the altar of your heart, and instead do what it takes to maintain intimate fellowship with him. God does not want you to go out and try to do things for him. He does not ask you to figure out what would be best for him and then set out on the task of accomplishing it. He simply wants your obedience.

Who is on the throne of your life? Is it God or your idols? Search your spirit for an honest answer. God is not to be toyed with. He will not tolerate sin. When God got Isaiah's attention by removing the idol in his life, King Uzziah, he became ready and desperate to see God. Then God revealed himself. He is an expert in taking care of all of the "Uzziahs" we put before him.

What an eye-opener it is when God reveals his pure, holy self to us and we see our idolatrous hearts for what they really are—dirty, filthy things God cannot tolerate. But he loves us, and he wants us to take that next step to renewing our relationship with him. He wants us to respond appropriately to his revelation.

CHAPTER FIVE

Revelation Response

I live in Oklahoma, which is part of an area of the United States that has rightly earned the nickname Tornado Alley. When spring severe weather begins to develop, our television meteorologists analyze their Doppler radar to predict the severity and track of the storm. They issue severe thunderstorm warnings and tornado watches as appropriate and send their videographers to the air so viewers can have a bird's-eye view of the storms. "Storm trackers" race to the area where the storm is developing so they can help spot tornados.

When a tornado is sighted, warnings are broadcast through every available means of communication, urging us to take immediate cover. These early warnings have saved countless lives. Of course, there are two ways of responding to a tornado warning: heed the warning and take appropriate shelter or ignore it. Smart people heed the warning; foolish ones ignore it.

God also has an early warning system: God's Doppler radar for the Christian life. We may be at the very point of temptation. Some person, thing, or opportunity is alluring to us, and we are contemplating taking sin's bait. These are initial thoughts and attitudes of sin—ones that seem to be involuntary reactions but if dwelt on or acted on would birth sin. At this point God tries to warn us to turn away before we actually venture into the sin. I call these convictions God's early warnings.

As with our local weather warning, Christians have two ways of responding: wisely or foolishly. Some of us are tuned in to hear the Spirit's early warnings, and we value them. We want that early nudge from the Spirit to stop us so we will turn from whatever is tempting us. Others, however, choose to ignore the warning signs and keep walking straight into the dangerous storm of sin.

For those who have *already* taken the bait and have let their hearts lust after other gods, God will use a four-step pattern to call them back from idolatrous living, as I've previously said.

Step 1 was God gets our attention. Step 2 was that he reveals himself to us in order to show us his holiness and our sin. But before revealing the third step of the pattern, I need to flesh out what I'm calling the "conduit" between steps 2 and 3. It's not something that can be packaged neatly into one step or the other, but it is a crucial aspect of moving someone to step 3 in God's progressive pattern. The conduit? Conviction.

Conviction

Jesus plainly told his disciples that one day he would leave them. But wanting to reassure them, he also told them he would send a Helper to them after he was gone, the Holy Spirit (John 14:16). This word *helper* comes from the Greek word *paraklētos*, which means "the one who stands by to help." In other words, the Holy Spirit is not just some passive bystander. He is a "stand-byer" who is there to actively help us.

Jesus also told the disciples about one of the specific duties of the Holy Spirit: conviction (John 16:7–8). The word *convict* in this passage has a very specific meaning. It means "to convince or to present evidence." In a courtroom trial, one party presents a long list of evidence for the purpose of convincing the jury that indeed a wrong has been committed.

The Holy Spirit works the same way in our lives. He presents evidence about our behaviors, thoughts, and attitudes to convict, or convince, us about sin and unrighteousness. Then he gives us the chance to respond.

The term *righteousness* from a biblical point of view has two aspects: our position and our practice. If we have repented of our sins and made a profession of faith in Jesus as our Savior, our position is that we are in Christ. The Holy Spirit places us in Christ at the moment of our salvation, and because of that we are righteous, or made right, before God. That is our position; it cannot change.

On the other hand, our practice, or our daily living, is not nearly as righteous (holy), as our position is. There is often a great gap between what God teaches us in his Word about how we should live our lives and how we actually live. The span of that gap between the two usually represents the depth of our maturity as a Christian. The more mature we are, the narrower the gap; the more immature, the wider the gap.

Therefore, the Holy Spirit works to narrow that gap by convicting us that our practice needs to be holy before God. Just as it is best to recognize and respond to God's discipline quickly, so it is with conviction. By learning to recognize ways the Spirit convicts us, we can become more sensitive to conviction and respond quickly.

One of the ways he convicts is through an inner voice speaking to us, telling us to walk away from something we shouldn't be doing. It might be like a check in our spirits, which should cause us to stop and examine our thoughts or actions. Or we may have a sense that what we're doing just feels wrong.

Another way the Holy Spirit convicts is by reminding us of truth. If we belong to Christ, no doubt there have been times in our lives when he has reminded us of what Scripture says about a particular attitude or action. For example, he may bring to mind a certain behavior and prompt us that it is contrary to God's will as recorded in the Bible. Or, when we're reading our Bible during daily devotions or working on a Bible study, a passage may have new relevancy to us in light of our current situation.

When that happens, God is trying to convince us that the action is wrong and will be destructive to us. That's also why it's so good for us to memorize Scripture, or at least be familiar with passages. He'll bring verses to mind when their truths are most applicable to us. Psalm 119:11 describes the benefit of this: "I have stored up your word in my heart, that I might not sin against you."

Sometimes the Holy Spirit sends people into our lives to confront us. It may be a pastor as he gives a message. Oftentimes congregation members tell me that I must have prepared a sermon just for them since it spoke so specifically to them. It's not me convicting them. It's the Holy Spirit convicting them through the preaching of the Word. The messages at Silver Cliff and the stewardship banquet are examples of God using a corporate message to convict multiple people at one time.

Maybe convicting confrontation will come from a Christian parent or friend. When a mature Christian approaches us with a concern about perceived sin in our lives, we should listen carefully and consider if what we are doing is a sin in God's eyes. While it is human nature to resist confrontation from another person, it may well be that the Lord is using that person to convict us.

The important thing is to develop a heart that's sensitive to the

Holy Spirit's convictions. When we're convicted, there is only one sincere response. The third step God leads us through to renew close fellowship with him is our response to conviction: *we confess and repent*. We confess and repent that we have let our hearts bow before something or someone other than the one true, holy God.

Confession

When we live in sin and don't deal with it, it weighs heavy on us and wears us down. In the thirty-eighth psalm, the psalmist laments the burden of sin in his life: "For my iniquities have gone over my head; like a heavy burden, they are too heavy for me" (v. 4). Sin consumes our emotional energy and leaves us spiritually depleted. I doubt there has ever been a person who entered into sin thinking it was going to be too much for them. But the longer we stay in it without repenting and turning to the Lord, the heavier the burden weighs on us. Confession is the cure for that burden.

The English word *confess* is the Greek word *homologeō*, which means "agreement." In this context, it describes when we come to the point of agreeing with God about a specific action or attitude. After we're convicted, we confess, or agree, that the action or attitude was wrong.

Unfortunately, Christians aren't often taught how to confess sins and many give surprisingly little thought to doing it. In fact, beyond confessing to being a sinner unworthy of God's grace at the time of their salvation, many would be hard-pressed to name other times they have intentionally confessed sins to God. Others might do well to occasionally toss in an oh-God-forgive-me-for-my-sins statement at the end of a prayer. Heartfelt confession, however, means we go much deeper to the level of identifying specific sinful actions, naming them before God.

For example, we might confess, "When I said such and such, when I went to that place, when I left that undone, when I viewed that on the computer, God, it was sin. I'm calling it the same thing you call it and seeing it as you do. I'm not justifying it anymore. I'm not trying to rationalize it, God. I want you to know that I know it is sin. God, thank you for letting me receive the forgiveness that is mine already in Christ."

Don't try to rationalize your sin; agree with God that it's sin. When people try to justify their actions, it sounds like, "I know it's wrong for most people to do it, but I'm only going to do it once." "Everyone else does it, so it can't be that bad." "It's just the way I am." "Oh, that's just me talking to myself; it's not God trying to convict me."

When John wrote, "If we confess our sins" (1 John 1:9), he was writing to believers. The word *if* in this verse means "if, and with all probability you will." This helps us understand that confession is not a one-time occurrence at the time of salvation; it is a recurring part of a healthy Christian life.

When I was a fairly new believer, I found myself confessing sins of *commission*, what I was doing but should not have been. These sins were obviously wrong. They embarrassed me, and I was ashamed of them. As I began to mature in the Lord, many of the sins of commission had ceased, so God began to convict me more of sins of *omission*, what I was not doing but should have been. My confession shifted more to sins such as a lack of prayer life, a lack of witnessing, a lack of sacrificial giving, and other shortcomings.

Now after many years as a "maturing" believer, I find myself more frequently confessing other types of sins, such as those of attitude. But I am no more comfortable with these sins in my life today than I was with those more outwardly obvious ones.

In the past I would pray, "God if there is any sin in my life, show it to me." While that's a great prayer and I'm convinced God answers that kind of prayer, I believe we need to graduate into deeper, more spiritually honest fellowship with God. I know there is sin in my life. Even if I don't readily recognize it, I sincerely want God to point it out to me. So now I say, "Lord, show me what you want to deal with next. I want to understand what it is in my life that's sinful and not pleasing to you."

Shame and Sorrow for Sin

Popular psychology tells us shame is a harmful emotion that is detrimental to one's self-image. But feeling shame for our sin is an important part of this third step of confession and repentance. It's true that shame can be destructive if we don't move beyond it, but feeling sorrow and shame for actions that hurt, disappoint, and displease God is appropriate and necessary.

At Silver Cliff, I saw many students express shame for sinful actions. When convicted, they became brokenhearted. Many called home and talked to their parents, tearfully asking forgiveness for things they had done to wrong them. I saw students talking with other students, remorseful for their actions and then rejoicing when they felt the air had been cleared between them and fellowship with each other—and God—had been restored.

On the other hand, I'll never forget one time when a very angry mother and father came to see me. Their teenage daughter had attended at least one worship service at our church and afterwards had told them she was ashamed about some of the things she had said and done in her life. The parents, who claimed to be members of another church but did not seem to be Christians, told me they had worked a long time to get their daughter past her feelings of shame. Now they were angry because after attending our church, their daughter said she was ashamed of some of her past behavior. They blamed me for this "terrible" circumstance. These parents had bought into humanism, and humanists say there is nothing we ought to be ashamed of.

The Bible, however, tells us differently and gives us several examples of individuals expressing shame for their actions. For example, Ezra, a godly Old Testament priest, prayed, "O my God, I am ashamed and blush to lift my face to you, my God, for our iniquities have risen higher than our heads, and our guilt has mounted up to the heavens" (Ezra 9:6).

Ezra had led the second group of Israelite exiles out of captivity in Babylon and back to Jerusalem. These people had fallen into great sin—specifically, intermarrying with pagan people and worshipping their gods. He was thoroughly ashamed of their behavior. Their sin was so repugnant to him that he described it as stretching up to heaven. But his shame was good in that it spurred him to positive action. He was instrumental in turning the people back to God.

What about the wayward son's shame? Luke tells us he turned away from his loving father to pursue idols of worldly pleasures and independence. After a while, this rebellious son found himself literally sitting in a pigpen clothed with the filthiness of his sin. Convicted of his squanderous lifestyle, he realized he had made a mess of his life and decided to return home. When the now-humbled son saw his father, he confessed, "Father, I have sinned against heaven and before you. I am no longer worthy to be called your son" (Luke 15:21). Oh, how he must have burned with shame as he stood before his father, admitting he had been so wrong.

Sorrow for sin should go hand in hand with shame for sin. Some people may be sorry because they get caught in their sin. Others may feel sorry because they're experiencing the pain of God's discipline or because they are suffering the consequences of their sin. But they're not yet sorry they participated in the sin. It's possible to have sorrow for sin and not repent, but it's not possible to truly repent without having sorrow for the sin.

The Bible gives us a particularly touching picture of sorrow for sin as a woman of ill repute encounters Jesus. Here's the scene how I picture it.

One evening Jesus was dining at a Pharisee's home. As was acceptable in that culture, several uninvited people lingered nearby. Some of these people may have watched him heal the sick earlier in the day and were just curious to see what he would do next. Others, like rubberneckers at the scene of an accident, may have stood around hoping to see more confrontation between Jesus and the Pharisees.

I believe one uninvited woman was there because she was inexplicably drawn to Jesus. She longed for healing that had nothing to do with physical healing. She stood there with her gaze riveted on Jesus, clutching a small vial of perfume in her hand. Was the perfume a gift for Jesus or just a trapping of her notorious profession that she happened to have with her?

She was sick of her sinful life and somehow knew this man held the power to help her change. Finally, she could stand it no longer. Her desperation gave her the courage to step out of the nighttime shadows. Pulling away from those who tried to hold her back, she went straight to Jesus and crumbled at his feet. She kissed them over and over again, a gesture of a humble servant who knelt before her Master and Lord. By this time she was sobbing uncontrollably. Her tears mixed with the perfume she was pouring on his feet, and she tried to wipe them dry with her hair. Then Jesus speaks to her. "Your sins are forgiven....Your faith has saved you; go in peace" (Luke 7:48–50).

I can't read that story without being so moved by her sorrow for her sin and her willingness to yield herself to the Lord. Do we ever, figuratively speaking, crumble at the feet of Jesus, overwhelmed with shame and sorrow for our sin? Do we love God so much that there have been times in our lives when it broke our hearts to think about how much our sin hurts him?

If we enjoy sin more than we enjoy fellowship with God, it should break our hearts. It means we haven't reached the point of becoming ashamed and broken about it. "The sacrifices of God are a broken spirit; a broken and contrite heart" (Ps. 51:17). God welcomes brokenness. When we come to fully realize how much sin hurts us, those around us, and the God we love, we should be sorrowful. If we don't ever feel brokenhearted about our sin, then we need to ask God to reveal it to us on a deeper level.

No, we should not dwell in shame and sorrow. Nevertheless, they are effective precursors to heartfelt repentance and renewed fellowship with God.

Repentance

Repentance is the companion to confession. One of the Greek words for repentance is *metanoeō*, which literally means "to change your mind about something." When we repent, we choose to stop participating in whatever we're repenting of. We turn away from it. We change our opinion about it. We not only become inwardly humbled by the recognition of our sin, we become outwardly and visibly changed by the experience of repentance. A truly repentant person will have no desire to take part in the sin again because of how much it hurts his or her heavenly Father.

Sometimes we don't actually want to give up the sin we're being convicted of. So we play the game of halfheartedly repenting. Compare it to the following scenario. Let's say I want to go to the top of the Empire State Building, but I also enjoy the security of being on the ground. So I put one foot in the elevator because I want to go to the top, but I leave the other foot firmly planted on the first floor. It's obvious what will happen. The elevator doors will just keep banging into me, and I will end up going nowhere. That's the frustrating picture of many Christians today. They say they want to experience God in a deeper way, but they keep one foot still firmly planted on the outside of his will.

People who say they have confessed sin to God, but who continue in the sin or quickly and easily fall back into it, have only halfheartedly repented of it. Don't be mistaken. God is not fooled nor pleased with halfhearted repentance. Truly repentant people make every effort possible, with God's help, to turn from the sin.

Hindrances to Repentance

I believe there is a startling lack of repentance among American Christians these days. In fact, there is a tremendous need today for wholehearted, sold-out, hold-nothing-back, brokenhearted repentance. Why is it that we do not regularly confess and repent of sin? We know that if we repent of sin God will restore the love relationship between us, that our lives will be blessed in the process, and that our Christian walk will be more satisfying. So why do we still do not do it?

The reasons are many, but I think pride is one of the major obstacles to repentance. Pride blinds us into rationalizing that what we are doing is not really sin. Therefore, we see no reason to repent. Repentance requires humility and submission to God; a prideful heart cannot be repentant. When we repent, we agree God is right and we are wrong. If we are unwilling to submit and obey, God will work to humble us while disciplining us to get our attention about the sin.

Ignorance can mask our sin too. By ignorance I mean we may not yet have learned that certain activities are sinful because we don't know what the Bible says about sin. This is biblical illiteracy, which happens most frequently to newer or less mature Christians who have not sat under biblical teaching for very long.

For example, God's Word says that gossip is a sin. But if we have not studied the Bible enough to recognize that gossip is clearly prohibited, then we will not know it is a sin. It's not a justifiable excuse for being a gossip, but it does help us understand how people can sin and not realize the significance of their actions. In society, ignorance of the law does not excuse us for breaking it, nor does ignorance of sin excuse us. Believers need to be life-long students of the Bible, learning firsthand about God's guidelines for living.

Sadly, other times we don't repent because we have become calloused toward the convictions of the Holy Spirit. As a young boy, I was fascinated by the thick calluses covering my father's palms, which he had earned from laboring in the construction business.

I could scrape his hand with a sharp object and he couldn't feel it. In the same way, every day that God reveals a sin in our lives, yet we rebuff him and refuse to turn from it, we add a layer of callus in our spirits.

Over time, we become accustomed and desensitized to the sin. The Spirit still convicts, but we can't feel his gentle nudges of conviction through the thick calluses in our spirit. Paul warns in 1 Thessalonians not to quench the Holy Spirit, and this is a perfect example of how that can be done. When it happens, God may have to progress through several types of discipline to get our attention, and only genuine repentance can remove our spiritual calluses.

Maybe we don't repent because we genuinely are not yet aware we are engaging in a particular sin. Sometimes the sin in my life has been obvious, and then other times I may have been involved in something I did not recognize as sin at first. A common symptom of this is when we experience dissatisfaction in our spiritual life. We sense something isn't right between God and us, but we just can't put our finger on why we feel that way. Unconfessed sin may be the problem. Ask God to reveal it. One of the most spiritually profitable ways we can spend our time is examining and opening our hearts before God.

The continual message of Jesus, from when he walked on earth to today, is one of repentance. "From that time Jesus began to preach and say, 'Repent, for the kingdom of heaven is at hand' " (Matt. 4:17). The verb tense here clearly tells us that Jesus did not say this only one time. He said it and just kept on saying it time after time after time. People may have gotten tired of hearing his message, but Jesus knew the importance of it. Repentance is not a one-time occurrence for believers.

As we continued our corporate study on idolatry in the months following the stewardship banquet, I saw repentance and changed behavior in many members. Some who had never tithed before told me they had been convicted to now tithe. Some donated money sacrificially to our building fund. Others volunteered for areas of service they previously would not have considered. And several confessed and turned from idols that had been eroding family relationships. It was wonderful to see how God changed their hearts and moved them to action.

"Thus says the Lord God: Repent and turn away from your idols, and turn away your faces from all your abominations" (Ezek. 14:6). God did not ask his people to merely feel ashamed of their idolatry or only to acknowledge their sin. He also issued a specific call to action: turn away from your sin. And in Joel he says, "return to me with all your heart" (2:12). *Return.* That's the most glorious aspect of repentance—breaking with the sin and returning to the fellowship of the Lord.

Isaiah's Revelation Response

"And I said: 'Woe is me! For I am lost; for I am a man of unclean lips, and I dwell in the midst of a people of unclean lips; for my eyes have seen the King, the Lord of hosts!' " (Isa. 6:5). When God revealed himself, all Isaiah could say is, "Woe is me!" He could have said, "Wow, God! This is a really awesome place," or "I must really be special since God let me visit the throne room of heaven." But those weren't his words. He was confronted with the stark contrast of his unholiness with God's absolute holiness. He was convicted of his sin, and his heart-felt response showed the depth of his shame.

We simply do not use the word *woe* anymore, except maybe jokingly, but the word means "despair, grief, distress, and sorrow." Isaiah's woeful response when he faced the sovereign and holy God was a statement of his overwhelming despair for his sinfulness.

First John 1:9 says that after we confess, Jesus will "cleanse" us from all unrighteousness. The word *cleanse* in the Greek language is *katharizō*, from which the English word *catharsis* comes. It means "purification or cleansing." God will completely remove every aspect of unrighteousness in our lives. What an incredible amount of peace and confidence we can have knowing that there is no obstacle between God and us.

The New Testament principle we live by today—that we are pure in God's eyes and forgiven of our sins when we repent—is graphically illustrated by what happens to Isaiah next. "Then one of the seraphim flew to me, having in his hand a burning coal that he had taken with tongs from the altar. And he touched my mouth and said: 'Behold, this has touched your lips; your guilt is taken away, and your sin atoned for'" (Isa. 6:6–7). What was the significance of the burning coal on Isaiah's lips? Purification. Extreme heat purifies and destroys contaminants.

It's like the autoclave my wife used when she worked as a surgical nurse. All of the instruments had to be sterilized in an autoclave, which is a device that uses high-pressure steam to destroy viruses, bacteria, and other contaminants. It was a way to "purify" the instruments.

When the seraph touched the burning coal to Isaiah's lips, it was a ritual of purification. It burned away, or forgave, his sins. The searing pain must have been unbearable as he repented of sin and surrendered the gods he had substituted for God in his life. If there is no pain or sorrow associated with our repentance, then we have to question the validity of it. Heartfelt repentance will bring tears and pain, but look at the wonderful result: pain yields to the joy and peace of purification and forgiveness.

Forgiveness

"I forgive you" are three of the sweetest words we can ever hear. I've seen them cause shouts of joy, bring tears of relief, wash away guilt, and change the course of lives. Conversely, when a parent, friend, or spouse withholds those words, the damage can be irreparable. As important as human forgiveness is, though, the most significant forgiveness we can ever receive comes from God.

The Bible describes two types of God's forgiveness. Theologians have coined the term *judicial forgiveness* for the forgiveness sinners receive when they first repent and trust Christ for salvation. They are justified—judged right with God by God. The result is that a new Christian receives an eternal relationship with God based on grace and forgiveness. This forgiveness is so complete that God removes our sin "as far as the east is from the west" (Ps. 103:12). If we have received Christ, God will never judge us for our sins. Every sin is already exposed to God's judgment through Christ's death (Ps. 130:4, Acts 26:18, Eph. 1:7, Col. 1:14). Our forgiveness is eternal; our relationship is permanent.

The other type of God's forgiveness, the one I'm primarily speaking of in this chapter, has to do with fellowship with God. It's appropriately called *fellowship forgiveness.* Let me stress that it has nothing to do with your relationship with God, as what was just described above. Think of fellowship forgiveness in the same way we would parental forgiveness.

For example, when a child rebels and is disobedient to the parent, the quality of the fellowship is diminished and the closeness of the relationship becomes strained. The parent is unhappy with the child and the child may feel guilty. But when a repentant child apologizes and asks for forgiveness, a loving parent will readily grant it. Then closeness in the relationship is restored. The child-parent relationship can't be severed, but the closeness can be affected. That's an example of fellowship forgiveness.

Do you realize the New Testament never actually tells us to ask for forgiveness? We're told to confess and repent, but we're not told to ask for forgiveness. Instead, as Christians we are to accept God's forgiveness that Christ died to provide us. Jesus died once for all of our sins. They have all been forgiven—past, present, and future. If we keep asking for forgiveness, it is as if we are asking Jesus to die again.

I've known some Christians who cannot seem to experience the joy of forgiveness. They punish themselves for years about a sin, confessing it numerous times but never believing God has actually forgiven them because they think they are too unworthy. They don't "feel" forgiven, so they can't believe God has really forgiven them. They are consumed by sins of their past and can't break free. Their sins haunt them relentlessly. That is not the will of God.

I am not belittling their feelings. I know at times a sin can become particularly difficult to reject. In the early part of the nineteenth century, these kinds of sin were called "besetting sins." They are those harassing temptations that cause us to feel as if we will never be able to break away from them. But the reality is Christ has set us free from permanent enslavement when he purchased us back from the slave market of sin with his blood on the cross. The problem is we may not experientially possess the freedom that is ours in Christ.

Once there was a man in my congregation who came to me and said, "Pastor, I'm going to have to resign as a deacon." When I asked why, he said, "Well, I committed an act of immorality and I cannot live with it any longer." I immediately assumed he had committed this act during the prior week so I said, "Let's pray together and let's confess it to the Lord."

"I've already done that," he said. When I asked him when the incident had happened, he told me it had occurred eighteen years ago. Now he was telling me he could not deal with it anymore. I asked him if he had confessed it to the Lord, and he replied, "Yes, I have. I have a thousand times. I have confessed it a thousand times a year for the last eighteen years!" His could not let it go, and it was driving him crazy. His story reminds me of the story of James Garfield, our twentieth president.

Less than four months after Garfield was elected president of the United States in 1880, a would-be assassin shot him in the back at a Washington, D.C., train station. Doctors searched for the bullet in the wound but could not locate it. The president was moved back to the White House, where a team of his personal doctors directed his care. Over and over again they probed the wound, desperate to find the bullet.

After many unsuccessful attempts, his doctors appealed for help from Alexander Graham Bell, who by that time had invented a device that worked much like a metal detector. They hoped it could help them locate the hidden bullet inside the president's body. Unfortunately, Bell's efforts failed too.

The president held on for a few months, but finally in September

1881 he died. He did not, however, die from the damage specifically caused by the bullet. Rather, poor care and complications of the blood poisoning caused by constant probing of unsterilized fingers in the wound killed him.[1]

Garfield's unfortunate demise reminds us that there comes a time when we have to stop the probing and say, "Lord, I am going to accept the forgiveness that is mine in Christ now and not deal with this thing again." Only more damage will be done if we keep probing and probing at the past sin.

You may still be probing a sin that you've previously confessed to God, but it is no act of faith to continue to confess sin God has already forgiven. God says when he forgives a sin, he forgets the sin. God doesn't "re-forgive" anybody. There's no such thing as re-forgiveness. When God forgives, he completely removes that sin. Even if you don't feel forgiven, by faith claim God's promise that you are and that he will restore your joyful fellowship.

Understand that Satan is the one who keeps bringing that sin to mind. He is the one who keeps planting seeds of doubt—not God. He is the one who whispers to you that your sin was so bad you don't deserve God's forgiveness.

Have you confessed your actions to God as sin? If so, then accept God's forgiveness and let go of them.

Recognizing Sin in Your Life

Satan, the great deceiver, will do all he can to encourage us to rationalize or justify our sin because he does not want us to recognize it for what it really is and to confess it. But unconfessed sin is dangerous to our spiritual health, so I challenge you to scrutinize your soul for it. Ask God to reveal your sin, and don't ignore the Holy Spirit's convictions when he does.

The most important question is, how will you respond? Recognizing it isn't enough. Confess it so you can turn your wandering heart back to God. The following questions can help you recognize unconfessed sin in your life:

(1) Is there a lack of fellowship or joy between you and God or you and your family? For example, your activity may be a sin if it is stopping your prayers from being effective. It may also be hurting your family.

(2) Do you decide if the lifestyle or action in question is a sin by comparing it to the lifestyle or actions of others? We can't look around at other people and say, "They get by with it; so can I" or "He's a Christian and he's doing it, so it must be okay."

(3) Do you judge whether an activity is sinful based upon your own opinion, temperament, or feelings? "It's just the way I am. I can't help it. I've always been this way," a guy told me one time. My thought was yes, he probably has been that way awhile—since he first fell into sin. Just because you don't "feel" like it is sin doesn't mean it isn't. Your feelings are not an impartial judge.

(4) Do you turn to God's Word to see what it says about your action (or lack of action)? It doesn't matter what you think should or should not be a sin. The Bible is the only measure against which to judge the activities of our lives. It is our guide for what is and is not sinful, and we must learn to consult it for clear instruction. While other godly people can counsel you about the nature of sin, we should accept their counsel only when it is clearly based upon Scripture. A plumb line for behavior has been established for us by God's loving grace, and that standard is the Bible.

When I read the Word of God and consider what it says, often the Holy Spirit will bring thoughts to my mind such as, "When you said that, it was a sinful act," or "When you went there, I was displeased." "I told you to do this, but you didn't obey." The promptings brought to mind are not based on my own opinion or the opinions of others but instead are convictions brought to mind from what God's Word says.

Commit to spend time with God in prayer and reading the Bible so he can speak to you about specific sins.

(5) Do you poll others to see what they think of your action? You can't judge a sin by the opinions of others. I've had Christians ask me, "Well, do you think it would be wrong for me to do this thing or that thing or the other thing? What's your opinion on it?" I tell them it doesn't matter what I think. It doesn't matter at all. It truly only matters what God thinks. Pray instead of asking others.

(6) Do you categorize sin and think you are not sinning because you are not engaging in the "big" sins such as murder, adultery, and theft? Attitudinal sins such as unforgiveness, impatience, fear, and lack of love are just as much sin. God calls us to look deeper—to deal with sins that aren't so obvious. Look for the root causes, the heart issues, of idolatry.

The Positive Message of Repentance

During my senior year in college, at great surprise to me, I was given the privilege of being a fellow in the religion department at my university. Early in the semester the chairman of the department gave me an assignment: write a research paper on what the Bible says about repentance.

After about two months, I brought him a very lengthy report, somewhat proudly thinking I had done a fine job on it. He looked at, thumbed through it, and said, "You haven't even scratched the surface." He handed it back to me. That same exchange happened four more times during the school year. It was almost the end of the year when, thoroughly humbled, I submitted my paper to him one last time. This time he said, "I believe you've finally begun to understand what repentance is about."

When he first gave me the assignment, I didn't like it. When I began to study it, I didn't like it. When I had to keep resubmitting the paper, I didn't like it. But now after thirty-five years of pastoring and getting to know the Lord better, I understand the wisdom of what that professor was trying to help me learn: one of the most important and positive truths of the Bible is the power of genuine repentance among the people of God. It is an essential element of maintaining fellowship with Christ. Christians must realize that before they can see prayers answered and God's power at work through their lives, there must be repentance.

When we are willing to repent, God will remove the obstacle of sin between us. Once again we will see God at work in our lives. He will continue to reveal himself to us, taking us into deeper, guilt-free fellowship with him. The dryness of a stagnant Christian life will begin to disappear, replaced with a more refreshing, vibrant fellowship.

CHAPTER SIX

Fellowship with the Father

The believer, God's precious child, is like a multi-faceted jewel. One facet may reflect the beauty of a believer's surrendered anticipation of God's Word. When the jewel is turned, the next facet reveals a faithful, trusting person whose perseverance in the ways of God have prepared the way for a closer walk with him. Rotate the jewel again and see that heartfelt, genuine repentance has removed the impediments that had fractured God's self-revelation. And radiating from the center of the jewel is intimate fellowship with the Father.

Christian, never lose sight of the reward of identifying idols in your life, repenting, and turning from them: close fellowship with God.

Fellowship with God doesn't have to be the elusive facet of the Christian life so many of us make it to be. Oftentimes believers will bemoan the fact they don't feel close to God. Although our relationship with God is not based on how we feel about it, our hearts should be sensitive enough that we can feel or sense when there is distance beginning to build between us and quickly discern the problem. And yes, close fellowship with God feels good.

As believers, our salvation involved more than us wanting to come to God. He called us to himself. This is the doctrine of election. There is only one way to come to God—through a personal relationship with Jesus Christ. Jesus said, "I am the way, and the truth, and the life. No one comes to the Father except through me." (John 14:6). God's call is not just a general call to a relationship with him, the only purpose of which is to assure you of eternal life in heaven. God's call is a call to personal fellowship—here and now in this life. We are created for fellowship with him.

Fellowship implies a two-way relationship. Think of it as two friends having a conversation and enjoying each other's company. Jesus used a wonderful metaphor of dining with us to describe this kind of fellowship. In Revelation, he dictated letters to the seven churches of Asia. One of the churches, Laodicea, was in a town of significant wealth and prestige located on a booming trade route between Ephesus and Syria. Unfortunately, this church, like churches do far too many times nowadays, had conformed to the society and norms of the city. They had allowed their hearts to wander from God to other gods and were serving self-interests instead of God.

First, Christ described the Laodicea church as "lukewarm" and sternly called for them to repent of their sins. He scolded them for becoming spiritually tepid, but then he offered them a wonderful word of encouragement: "Behold, I stand at the door and knock. If anyone hears my voice and opens the door, I will come in to him and eat with him, and he with me" (Rev. 3:20).

In the culture of that day, spending time eating with someone was a very personal and mutually honoring time. The Laodicean side of the relationship had become lukewarm, but Jesus still longed to have fellowship with them. If they would just repent and turn back to him, he promised they could dine with him again—in other words, fellowship together and enjoy each other's presence.

In the Presence of God

What does it mean to be in God's presence? It's kind of a vague phrase that's more commonly used than commonly understood. Theologically, we know God is omnipresent. He is everywhere all the time, including with us at this very moment, so in that sense, we're always in his presence.

There were times God made his presence known in tangible ways during Old Testament Bible times. For example, in Genesis he appeared in an anthropomorphic (taking on human attributes) form in the Garden of Eden and walked with Adam. In Exodus, he revealed himself as a cloud during the day and a pillar of fire at night to lead the Israelites as they wandered in the desert. Also in Exodus, Moses saw God in a burning bush that was not consumed by the fire. But instances such as these are not what I mean when I refer to entering into the presence of God today.

Jesus taught where two or three are gathered together in his name, he would be in their midst (Matt. 18:20). This does not mean he would reveal his glorious presence manifested in one of the ways described above. Instead, it means there was a deliberate recognition that those gathered had come before the Lord as a group of believers.

Individually, when we come into the presence of God, we stop our preoccupation with calendars, cell phones, e-mail, and other distractions to deliberately recognize our God who is always with us. The omnipresent God becomes the focus of our immediate worship and peace. We communicate with him. If we give him our time and undivided attention, he will draw us into a special time of fellowship during our prayer, Bible study, and worship times.

We also practice his presence by thinking of him throughout

the day, picturing him at our side and watching everything we do. We make a conscious effort to live like we know he's there with us. We want to please him by our lifestyle.

Eighteenth-century minister Robert Murray McCheyne described a believer's desire for the presence of God this way:

> A believer longs after God—to come into His presence, to feel His love, to feel near to Him in secret, to feel in the crowd that He is nearer than all the creatures. Ah! dear brethren, have you ever tasted this blessedness? There is greater rest and solace to be found in the presence of God for one hour, than in an eternity of the presence of man.[1]

Have you ever been around people who exemplify this? A man who was a longtime pastor and a mentor to me was like that. Even if I was around him for just a little while, I knew I had been with somebody who had been with Jesus. Unfortunately, he was a rarity. From my experience, I can tell you that most Christians spend little time in the presence of God, nor do many take the steps to remedy the situation.

I was a believer many years before anybody ever taught me how to approach God and spend time in his presence. How I wish someone would have taught me how to years earlier. To experience the presence of God, we need to prepare to do so. The Old Testament gives us one example of how to do this.

Entering the Presence of God—Old Testament Style

There is much we can learn from the early Israelites' worship. God gave meticulous instructions on how to build and furnish the temporary tabernacle, and later the permanent temple (Ex. 40 and other Old Testament references). He also gave detailed instructions about how they were to worship him. The Old Testament worship in the tabernacle offers a wonderful demonstration of preparing our hearts to come into the presence of the Lord.

The tabernacle had three divisions: the outer court, the Holy Place, and the Holy of Holies. As the name suggests, the outer court made up the outside perimeter surrounding the tabernacle tent. The brazen altar, on which sacrifices were burned, and the laver, which held water for the priests and worshippers to wash with, were both in the outer courtyard. Here worshippers performed the first preparatory steps of worship. They confessed and repented of sin, washing at the laver to symbolically cleanse themselves of sin. They also gave the priests the animals they had brought for sin offerings.

Inside was an area called the Holy Place. It contained a table of showbread (bread representing the twelve tribes of Israel and God's willingness for fellowship and communion), an ornate golden candlestick (lighting the way to God as Jesus does for us now), and an altar of incense (a symbol of the sweet fragrance of the prayers going up to God). In the Holy Place priests made a final preparation of their hearts to come before God in the Holy of Holies.

The most inner place, the Holy of Holies, contained the Ark of the Covenant, which held the Ten Commandments. More importantly, though, the very presence of God, the *Shekinah* glory, dwelt here. A thick veil separated the Holy Place from the Holy of Holies. Only the Jewish high priest could enter into the Most Holy Place.

Once a year on the Day of Atonement the high priest would atone for sins on behalf of all of God's people. First, he symbolically repented, cleansed himself, and offered a sacrifice in the outer courtyard. Only after performing this ritual would the high priest enter the Holy Place, where he would further prepare his heart and mind to approach God.

Finally, he would go behind the veil into the Holy of Holies, literally entering into the presence of God on behalf of the people. The high priest would take the blood that had been collected from the sacrificial animals and pour it on the mercy seat, which was above the Ark of the Covenant. This act symbolically covered over the sins of the people. Jews call this Yom Kippur (see Leviticus 16).

Approaching God Today

Today, Christians can worship and approach God in a far superior way than that of the Old Testament. We are a New Testament church and people. We are no longer under the law and required to follow exact and elaborate steps of worship. Believers now have direct access to God through Christ's death on the cross:

> Therefore, brothers, since we have confidence to enter the holy places by the blood of Jesus, by the new and living way that he opened for us through the curtain, that is, through his flesh, and since we have a great priest over the house of God, let us draw near with a true heart in full assurance of faith, with our hearts sprinkled clean from an evil conscience and our bodies washed with pure water (Heb. 10:19–22).

Now let's examine the key phrases of this passage.

"Enter the Holy Places"

We can go through the outer Holy Place to the place where God's presence dwelled—the Holy of Holies. As believers in Christ, we can confidently come before God.

The Creator of the universe.

The Sovereign of all time and space.

The one who existed before anything else existed.

The one who spoke everything into existence.

The one who made the majesty of the mountains and the serenity of the seas.

The one who was able to establish the intricacies of the atom.

The one who has been in charge of history, from the beginning to the end.

The one for whom everything exists.

The one who loves you more than anyone has ever loved you.

He is the eternal God who is absolutely, completely holy. He is limited only in the fact that he has chosen never to break his attributes or his character. Apart from that, he is the completely unlimited God and the only absolutely pure being. He has chosen to reveal himself to us in everything he has made and to reveal himself to us in Jesus.

You and I can come into the presence of that God! I hope the sheer magnitude of that amazing privilege is something you never take for granted. Never let it become mundane. I pray you never lose your respect for what it means to be in his presence.

In our own power, authority, and strength, we can never come into the presence of God. If you are in Christ, however, you have the privilege of coming into his presence and can do it with confidence. You don't have to sneak in. You don't have to wonder if you are welcome. You belong there because you are in Christ.

"New and Living Way"

When we approach God and enter his presence with confidence, it is only through one path: "by the blood of Jesus, by the new and living way" (vv. 19–20). The word *new* is a word that refers to a freshly slaughtered animal, which makes the word *living* remarkable.

Think back to the tabernacle experience. The priest could not enter into the Holy of Holies without killing an animal and bringing its blood to the mercy seat. Believers have a substitutionary sacrifice that is living—Jesus Christ. We approach God by the authority of the sacrificial Lamb of God, Jesus, who was the final and perfect sacrifice to atone for our sins. Jesus is this "new and living way" and is the one who initiated this new and living way of approaching God.

"Through the Curtain"

The permanent temple in Jerusalem had a very thick curtain to shield the people from God's presence just as the temporary tabernacle did. When Jesus was crucified on the cross, the earth shook, rocks were split, and the veil of the temple was torn in two from top to bottom, symbolizing from that point forward forever God's children could approach him directly instead of having to go through a priest (Matt. 27:51).

Today there still exists a "curtain" separating mankind and God, keeping man out of the presence of God. Only now it is not a thick curtain. Instead, it is the person of Jesus himself. When we accept Jesus as Lord and Savior, we pass "through the curtain" (v. 20) to God. Every time we come into the presence of God, we need to know that we are there because of only one thing: we have passed through Jesus by faith.

In effect, Jesus, the great High Priest, takes us by the hand and presents us to his Father. Isn't that a beautiful thought?

"Draw Near"

This passage also shows how we are given a choice. We can choose to come into the presence of God—or not. Therein lies the problem. Sadly, many Christians do not choose to do so. When was the last time you deliberately decided to approach and meet with him? You may say in response, "Well, you know, this afternoon I prayed to God and asked him to do this, that, and the other thing." While there is nothing wrong with praying for God to meet your needs, there is something wrong with desiring to approach God in that way only.

Try going to God with no ulterior motives. Most of our prayers commence out of a desire to get something from God rather than simply to worship in his presence. We ask for his protection, his help, or his blessing, but he deserves a lot more than that. If the only time you desire his presence is to ask him for something, then you are missing the point of prayer.

This Hebrews passage says "let us draw near" (v. 22). James says the same thing, but he also adds some incredibly reassuring words: "Draw near to God, *and he will draw near to you*" (James 4:8, emphasis added). What an amazing promise.

"In Full Assurance"

By faith, we know we are in the presence of God and have complete certainty about it because he has told us this in his Word. That is the full assurance of faith.

"Our Hearts Sprinkled Clean"

The last thing in the world that the Old Testament high priest would have ever done in the tabernacle was to go into the Holy of Holies with any known sin in his life. It meant death if he did. Therefore, he was very thorough and deliberate in preparing his heart and confessing sin. The high priest had no doubts about what was expected of him, and he prepared himself before entering exactly according to God's instructions. He knew he had to be sin-free to stand before God.

When we prepare our hearts to meet with an absolutely holy God by confessing and repenting of all sin first, we have confidence to approach God because "our hearts [are] sprinkled clean from an evil conscience and our bodies washed with pure water" (v. 22).

Imagine Yourself in the Temple

Remembering the divisions of the temple and practices of the Old Testament worshippers helps remind us of the seriousness of approaching God—that doing so is not something to be treated casually. Additionally, it's yet another reminder there simply is no way to have close fellowship with God if we don't regularly take the time to examine our lives and confess our sins.

Particularly for those who sometimes say they just don't feel forgiven for a past sin, being more deliberate about confessing and coming to God can help move them beyond that feeling.

Imagining yourself entering the temple is a very personal way to prepare your heart for fellowship with your heavenly Father. Please understand that I'm not talking about some strange, New Age self-hypnosis or contemplative spirituality. What I am saying is it can be helpful to consider what the Bible tells us about the practice of the Old Testament Jews, and then apply the principles of worship, respect, and reverence for the holiness of God. Take a few minutes to try it now and repeat it often on your own.

First, with eyes of faith walk through the tabernacle gate into the courtyard. Imagine you are walking on holy ground. Remember the sacrifice Jesus made for you on the cross as you gaze at the brazen altar of salvation. It was his blood that made atonement for your sins. Thank God for giving Jesus as our sacrifice. If you have never accepted Jesus Christ as Lord and Savior, you can do so right here at the brazen altar. Confess with your mouth Jesus is your Lord, and believe God raised him from the dead.

Next, picture yourself stepping to the laver and symbolically washing away your sins by confessing, repenting, and accepting God's forgiveness. Tear down the idols you've put before God. Ask him to reveal sin in your life and confess it. Be honest with him. Don't rationalize your sin. Don't justify it. Simply say, "God, I agree with you. I desire to turn from my sin." If he reveals something to you that you don't want to let go, remember that sin is what is keeping you from the deeper fellowship with God you desire.

After you've confessed and repented, imagine yourself walking into the Holy Place, where you will further prepare your heart and mind for the presence of God. Anticipate what it will be like when you stand before him.

Now see yourself walking alongside Jesus, your High Priest, stepping through the torn curtain. Feel free to do what you would do if you were walking into heaven and coming face-to-face with God. What would come naturally to you? Would you fall to your knees? Praise him and thank him? Would you be intimidated on that day?

Don't be intimidated now. Allow yourself to meet with him, praise him, and thank him for all he has done.

Don't ask for anything. Do you think the first thing on your mind would be, "Oh, God, I need a few more sales this month"? Would you be saying, "God, my back's hurting," or "My kids are acting up," or "God, I've got to meet with my boss tomorrow, and I'm afraid"? Don't you think being in the presence of God would be such an awesome experience that you would have something more to say than "Gimmee, gimmee, gimmee"? There is nothing wrong with asking God for something, but I don't think that would be the first thing on your mind.

Talk to him about your family; name them by name. What is your heart burdened with? Ask him to mend relationships and families. Bring requests for your church to God. Ask him to help you and others in the church love one another in the way we should and to pursue him, putting him first before tradition or anything else. Pray for your pastor and other church leaders to provide biblical church leadership and to be protected from Satan's attacks. Ask God to manifest himself in your body of believers in a marvelous way and to send spiritual renewal.

Then turn to your own spiritual condition. Ask God to do a new work in your own life and to draw you closer to him than you have ever been before. If you've truly prepared your heart, you are standing before him without sin. That is his promise. Ask him to help you lay down those distractions, doubts, and attitudes that distort your fellowship with him. Perhaps bitterness, fear, some character flaw, or something else is keeping you from having the fulfilling spiritual life he wants you to have. Ask him to help you lay them down and to move on.

Finally, simply bask in his presence. Fellowship with God is a two-way relationship. From God's perspective, he takes pleasure in us and is literally blessed by us as we seek to fellowship with him. From our perspective, we find peace, meaning, strength, joy, and purpose. The psalmist says, "in your presence there is fullness of joy" (16:11). Don't rush; give God your worship by spending time with him.

Fellowship Is Vital

Let's step back a minute and take a broad view of what's been said. Fellowship with God is vital for believers. I believe we hear too much preaching and teaching about the salvation event of coming to Christ, and not enough about growth and fellowship with Christ. The very weakest point of our relationship with Jesus should be the moment of our salvation. At that point, we are brand new babies in Christ. We don't have any spiritual maturity since the Holy Spirit hasn't had much time to teach us his ways. There haven't been many opportunities for us to see God work in our lives, and we haven't had time to learn to trust him through lots of different, daily experiences. We have not had time to really grow and get to know him. But we should be progressing and maturing in our relationship with God from the point of salvation on.

It's like a good marriage relationship. If you've been married several years, hopefully over time you and your spouse have grown closer and more in love with each other. The relationship has matured and the knowledge of each other's desires, dislikes, and goals has grown. The best time in your relationship should not have been the day you were introduced to one another.

What about your relationship with Jesus? Do you love him more, and are you more intimate in your walk with him today than you were last year at this time? Are you regularly repenting of sin? Have you come to grips with what Christ has done and who he is? With what we have done and who we are—sinners saved only by God's grace?

It's a sobering fact many people do not know Jesus and do not have any heart to know him, but it is even sadder when a believer turns away from pursuing to know him better. If that describes your relationship with him, then you need to ask why.

As human beings we were created with this wonderful capacity to both worship God and be a friend of God. We worship him for the incredible holy being that he is, but we can also enjoy close fellowship with him as a friend. It is natural for Christians to desire intimacy with Christ. Obeying, pleasing, and being faithful to him give us great satisfaction.

When we understand biblical truths, confess our sins, pray with passion, and serve God effectively, we have a sense of expectancy and peace that is hard to describe. We cannot let our feelings subjectively determine how close we are to God; nevertheless, knowing you are right with God offers a source of pleasure and peace like none other. Don't become complacent about those times when our connection with God seems to be remote, cold, or quiet.

But what is the purpose of intimacy with Christ? Do we seek it because we are myopic and egocentric, in other words for what it can do for us? Is it our fix, like what an addict seeks from a mind-altering drug? If that's our concept of intimacy with Christ, we've missed the point. God isn't working to provide us with some novelty. There are much deeper and more important issues. Intimacy points us to glorifying Christ by cooperating with his mission.

As Spirit-filled Christians we are called to *practice* the presence of God. Our faith should be evidenced by our works (James 2) while we perform our ordinary activities and encounter people in ordinary situations of work, family, and public interactions.

We were all made for the purpose of glorifying God. Fellowship helps us to fulfill our intended purpose and to experience joy in our daily lives, regardless of our circumstances. It is the engine that drives us to worship God and to serve him.

CHAPTER SEVEN

Called to Be a Disciple

How sad it is that many Christians never hear God call them to serve. Though that's the painful truth, the question is, why don't they? Most likely it is because they have become content to live with sin in their lives. They choose to ignore it, they don't repent of it, and thus, their stagnant spiritual life has become status quo.

As long as Isaiah lived in his sin, he had no word from God. He did not hear God calling him to do anything. But when Isaiah came to the place in his life where he had no gods but God, his heart was open to hear his call: "Then I heard the voice of the Lord, saying, 'Whom shall I send, and who will go for us?'[1] Then I said, 'Here am I. Send me!' " (Isa. 6:8).

Sometimes, little words carry big meanings. We tend to skip over them and miss the full intent because we're not paying attention. Make sure you notice the word *then* in that verse. After God got Isaiah's attention about his wayward heart, after he glimpsed the holy God, after he understood the importance of confessing sin to remove obstacles standing in his way of deeper fellowship with God, then and only then did he stand ready to make himself available in God's service. God offered Isaiah a chance to make a difference and not live consumed with self. Isaiah did not hesitate. "I am here, ready to serve you; use me." He was willing to be sent on a mission of service for his Lord.

And that is the final step of God's four-step pattern of calling our hearts back to him: *God calls us to engage in his service as dedicated disciples.*

If we yield ourselves to Christ, are obedient to him, and maintain intimate fellowship with him, we will have a unique dimension of God's presence to accomplish any task he asks of us. Like Isaiah, a repentant Christian's heart is a broken heart—one that is humbled before the sovereign, almighty God. A unique thing happens when a person is broken before the Lord. Jesus says, "I am going to pick you up. I'm going to use you now. You can fully worship me now because I have your heart."

Go: Missional Living

Jesus gave his disciples these final instructions before he departed earth: "Go therefore and make disciples of all nations, baptizing them in the name of the Father and of the Son and of the Holy Spirit, teaching them to observe all that I have commanded you" (Matt. 28:19–20). This verse is known as the Great Commission.

The word *go* in this verse was not in the imperative tense in the original language of the Bible. It wasn't a command: "Go!" as in get going, depart, get out of here. In this context go has more of a continuous nature. Jesus is telling his disciples that as they are going through life, they are to make disciples of all people of all ethnic groups and races. We've coined a term today for what Jesus was describing: *missional living.*

That term may bring to mind a picture of traditional missionaries—men and women who leave home and travel some distance to engage people with the gospel. Indeed, church history is filled with people such as Lottie Moon, Hudson Taylor, and

Adoniram Judson who traveled far away and endured terrible hardships to share Christ with indigenous people groups. Today, there are thousands of vocational Christian missionaries serving throughout the world. We applaud and pray for them, but the fact is, every Christian is called to be a missionary. It would be accurate to say if you are a Christian, you are a missionary.

All believers are called to serve on the mission field among our own families, neighbors, coworkers, friends, and acquaintances. We do not have to ask God for a special word to direct us to this mission. It is already spelled out for us in the Bible. Right where we are while engaging in our typical, daily activities we are to be in the process of making disciples, baptizing them in the name of the Father, the Son, and the Holy Spirit, and then teaching them to do what Jesus taught us. This isn't a new concept; Jesus introduced it nearly two thousand years ago.

The bottom line of this vital biblical truth is this: as Christians, we all are to adopt the lifestyle, thinking, and behavior of a missionary and engage the people who are interwoven throughout our lives in spiritual conversations. Our overall mission is to explain the gospel in a clear and compelling way. No matter what your age, experience, or personality, you are called to missional living; it's what people who are disciples of Christ do. And it's the primary mission of the church.

Ordinary People

You might be thinking, "Not me. How could God use me? I have no special abilities. I don't know enough about the Bible to teach others. I might say the wrong thing." It's easy to fall into the trap of thinking we have no special talents or knowledge and that God could not possibly want to use us. But do you know what that kind of thinking is? It's simply one of the many lies Satan uses to try to halt the work of Christ.

The Bible is filled with examples of ordinary people who, after submitting to God's purpose and being filled with his Spirit, served God in amazing ways. Look at the men Jesus chose to be his closest confidants and disciples. They were ordinary men; most were common laborers. One was a tax collector, which was a position his fellow Jews despised. These men had been going about their usual, daily work when Jesus called them to join him on his earthly mission. Later, God used these men for the mission of powerfully preaching the gospel and establishing the Christian church.

The story of a familiar Bible character begins with, "In the fifteenth year of the reign of Tiberius Caesar, Pontius Pilate being governor of Judea, and Herod being tetrarch of Galilee, and his brother Philip tetrarch of the region of Ituraea and Trachonitis, and Lysanias tetrarch of Abilene, during the high priesthood of Annas and Caiaphas..." (Luke 3:1–2). That's quite a list of impressive people. It's also the kind of passage we tend to skip over. We regard it as uninteresting background information we will not remember, standing in the way of the important stuff. But don't go too fast. The fact that we are told about these people has more significance than just giving us scene-setting information.

Suffice it to say that all of the people listed in these verses were powerful men and the highest officials in the land. These politically influential figures had the means to accomplish great feats, yet God did not choose any of them for the important mission he had in mind. After the list, we find these simple words: "the word of God came to John." Don't fail to see that God used an unrecognized person to accomplish the great work that needed to be done. He enlisted John the Baptist to prepare people for the coming of his son, Jesus.

John's preparation for his task was unlike that of the disciples and quite different from how anyone would think God would prepare someone for ministry.

Preparation in the Desert

As the son of a priest, most likely John would have been educated at the best Jewish schools by the smartest scholars, if God had not had other plans for him. Instead, God chose to send him to a different learning environment: the "College of the Desert."

I grew up in Phoenix, and my home was literally next to the desert. I love the desert. I think it is beautiful, and I enjoy taking photographs of the desert scenery. Also, one of my favorite hobbies is "jeeping" in the desert. But I fully understand how dangerous the desert can be. Its relentless heat saps your energy and can create such an intense thirst that it leaves no room to focus on anything but survival by satisfying that thirst. Unsatisfied thirst means death. The desert stretches for rough, lonely miles in all directions. In the Arizona desert, it's not uncommon to see a rattlesnake or Gila monster, the only poisonous lizard in the United States.

John learned several lessons in the desert—ones still good for us today. In chapter 2, we were warned how our four basic desires— to be loved, to have security, to enjoy life's pleasures, and to be significant—can become idols. But John didn't let these desires become his idols. Instead he relied on God to fulfill them.

First, I believe John clearly knew God loved him. No doubt his parents would have often told him the story about how God had blessed them in their old age with a son—a son who was chosen by God for a specific mission. Not only did an angel foretell of his birth, but the angel's prophetic message also included his name. Being told of God's special attention on him down to choosing his name before his birth had to make John feel loved and secure.

Also, John learned to depend on God for his basic needs such as the water and food that naturally would be quite scarce in the desert. God also protected him from the dangerous heat, insects, and animals. His security and safety were in God's hands.

Furthermore, in the desert John wasn't distracted by desires for unnecessary pleasures. He endured the tough, desert environment that in no way would have been considered pleasant living conditions. I imagine Satan tried to tempt John to leave the desert and return to the city to an easier life. He probably reminded him about the house, family, friends, and good food he had left behind. Satan may have told him it was unreasonable for God to have made him live like this and that surely God wouldn't mind if he left the desert a little early. But John persevered until God called him out of the desert to begin his ministry.

Perseverance, or endurance, may be the greatest Christian quality of all. It may also be one of the most difficult and sometimes-painful character traits for us develop. But the result is that God then has workers who do not get sidelined by every little trial that comes along. Instead, there is sufficient maturity in us to have faith that God has the desire and power to see us through whatever we have to face.

Paul said, "Not only that, but we rejoice in our sufferings, knowing that suffering produces endurance, and endurance produces character, and character produces hope" (Rom. 5:3–4). Character is not the outside facade that is visible to everyone. It is not the mask covering the real person. Instead, it is what we are deep down inside. It births what we do when we think nobody is looking. It is the foundation for all actions, attitudes, and words of our lives. Perseverance builds our character; proven character brings hope— the faith that purpose and joy will come after the trial.

As John persevered in the desert, the hope of the coming Messiah for whom he was to prepare the way and the knowledge that he had a God-given purpose kept him going. Likewise, as we spiritually mature and our character is adapted and conformed to God through trials, we will have confidence and hope for tomorrow. And we will have learned that the same God who saw us through trials in the past can be trusted to see us through the trials of today.

God often allows adversity in our lives, just as he did John's, in order to teach us important lessons of dependence and obedience. We may not understand why the trials are happening in our lives, but if we learn to depend on Jesus and his truths through them, then they will have been worth it. Our trials may be given to us specifically to prepare us for a work we can't even imagine at this point. But each day's common experiences, the struggles we endure, and the people God puts in our paths contribute to our preparation. Only in hindsight can we piece together how past experiences were providentially woven together to prepare us for today's God-ordained task.

Lastly, John did not let love for significance become an idol for him. One-on-one with God in the desert, he was driven to seek only God's favor. In the desert quiet, he developed a sensitive ear to God's voice and cherished close fellowship with his heavenly Father. Most of us struggle to get alone, and when we are alone, we're uncomfortable. We fight so many distractions. We can't seem to discipline ourselves to get away from phones, e-mail, Facebook˚, television, to-do lists, and kids long enough to listen for God's voice. Oblivious to the problem, we wonder why we do not hear from him. Jesus said, "My sheep hear my voice" (John 10:27), but we have to remain still for long enough to listen for his voice.

Later as John began his ministry, he was not tempted to look to men to validate or promote it, to seek applause from the crowds, or to try to build his own ministry. He already understood that his significance and purpose was rooted in pleasing and serving God not men. He kept firmly focused on his mission.

Romans 8:28 tells us that God can use every experience in our lives to encourage our conformity to the image of Christ. And through the pain, he can draw us closer to him. So for those of you desert-dwellers who are in a season of suffering, quit kicking the sand and cursing the sun. Savor the heat. In the heat of the desert we have a chance to grow much stronger in our faith and deepen our intimacy with God.

Becoming a Disciple

Jesus' words in the Great Commission were literally spoken to the twelve disciples, but his instructions to go, make disciples, baptize, and teach are for anyone who is a disciple of Christ. The definition of disciple is "one who accepts and assists in spreading the doctrines of another."[2] A disciple of Jesus is one who is committed to learning from Jesus, growing to be like him, and applying what he says to his or her life—at home, at work, and in every other aspect. Any of us who meet those criteria can be called a disciple of Jesus. For the rest of our lives on this earth, God is going to be at work creating in us a heart to become a disciple—a fully devoted learner and follower of Jesus who is ready and willing to serve him.

There are actually two disciple-related issues for us. First, we are to become disciples, and secondly, we are to make disciples. We have to become followers of Christ by experiencing God's salvation through repentance of sin and acceptance of Christ's atonement on the cross before we can disciple anyone else. After that, however, our efforts to grow individually as a disciple and our efforts to make disciples run on parallel paths. From the moment of our salvation, though, we are qualified to tell others about what Jesus has done for us.

When Jesus began his public ministry, he called twelve men to be his close disciples. For three years these men joined him in ministry as he taught and trained them to continue his work after he was gone. They spent copious amounts of time together as they actively served with him in his ministry.

Think about what Jesus did during the three years he had to train the disciples. What special characteristics did he try to mold in these men so that he trusted them with the gospel message? Are we striving to gain those characteristics? What can we learn from their example that will help us make disciples of others?

Learn from the Perfect Example

First of all, disciples looked to Jesus, the perfect teacher, as their example and so should we. Read the Bible stories about him, study the parables he told, learn the principles for righteous learning he taught, and observe how those around him reacted. We are to emulate Christ—not our favorite pastor, teacher, or any other person.

Become a Student

The disciples were students. No doubt they already knew many of the Old Testament Scriptures from their Jewish upbringing. But now they were being asked to learn a whole new way of thinking that was contrary to their Jewish, legalistic teachings and apply it to daily life. Jesus challenged them and stretched their thinking.

The Bible is the primary God-ordained tool for equipping believers for his work. Regularly attend a good Bible-teaching and preaching church. Sign up for a Bible study. Read the Bible and discuss how to apply it to your life. "All Scripture is breathed out by God and profitable for teaching, for reproof, for correction, and for training in righteousness" (2 Tim. 3:16).

Over the years I've seen the members of our church grow in their desire to study the Scriptures more deeply. In fact, our church has become known as a "teaching" church, as we've strived to take our members to a deeper level of biblical knowledge and understanding. Quite simply, effective disciples are life-long students of the Bible.

Pray

"Activism militates against your prayer life," a friend of mine used to say. It's far easier for us to be "doers" than "pray-ers." Instead of taking matters into our own hands, however, our first step should be to stop and pray. How many of us often skip that invaluable first step?

Jesus prayed. Of all of the people in the world who shouldn't have to pray, Jesus would be at the top of my list. He is the Son of God. He knows the Father intimately and personally, and he has known God throughout all eternity. Yet, as we study Jesus' life, we find him often retreating to places where he could be alone to pray. Jesus exemplified a life of prayer. Why? Because he knew the source of his power while living on earth depended upon his relationship with his heavenly Father, and he wanted his disciples to learn that same lesson.

Jesus also taught his disciples to pray for God to meet their needs. In one instance, Jesus told them to "pray earnestly to the Lord of the harvest to send out laborers into his harvest" (Matt. 9:38).

E. M. Bounds, an eighteenth-century minister, prayer warrior, and author, described prayer as a trade to be learned with much practice and care. How true. Prayer is work, requiring discipline and practice.

Many times I've asked a group of Christians this question, "How many of you are really happy with your prayer life?" Do you know how many raise their hands? None. And I can't raise my hand either because I'm not satisfied with my prayer life. I'm praying more than I have ever prayed in my life, and still I sense it isn't enough. I hope you will never be satisfied with your prayer life, either.

There is no excuse for not pursuing a deeper prayer life. Of course, there's no need to keep a stopwatch and time ourselves either. "Okay, God, I'm going to start praying right now. Let's see…okay, I've prayed for thirty-three seconds!" In no way am I suggesting we determine the success of our prayer life by the length of time we pray. But if we don't spend sufficient time with God in prayer, we will shortchange our lives, as well as those around us.

One of the screen savers on my computer is a marquee that says, "I will accomplish more by my prayer life than anything else I do." I've seen God do more in my children's lives in direct relationship to Marcia's and my prayers for them than anything else we have done. It's true in our marriage as well. I prayed the Lord would give Marcia and me a deep relationship with him and with each other, and I prayed God would make her into a spiritual giant. God has graciously answered those prayers.

Prayer is an incredible privilege for Christians. It is our connection to God. It is in our prayer life that we are granted time to commune with our sovereign Lord. Prayer allows us to access the greatest power of the Christian life, and a disciple needs to have a concentrated and deep prayer life.

Spread the News

Many Christians spend a great deal of their time trying to justify the fact that they are not willing to speak to the people around them about Jesus—the very thing all believers are called to do. But disciples tell others about Jesus. When people tell me they are not qualified to talk to someone about Jesus or that they do not know the Bible well enough to share what it says, I want to say, "Well why not? Why don't you study the Bible? Why don't you sign up for classes that teach you how to share your faith? Why don't you devote time to learning God's Word?"

God has providentially placed us in the lives of people (yes, I understand some of them may be very difficult people) so that we will *speak* the truth of the gospel to them. I know it is not easy. It is challenging to tell your neighbors about God. Maybe your neighbors don't go to church. Maybe they're not very nice and it's hard to be civil to them.

I've had people tell me, "My life communicates what God wants said, so I don't actually have to talk to people about God." I don't agree, and the Bible says God doesn't either. Although it is true that your lifestyle can speak volumes, good or bad, living a Christian lifestyle is not enough. God wants to use us to speak the truth in love to others. If the disciples had not been willing to tell people about Jesus, Christianity would have died in the first century.

Some people admit they're afraid they'll say the wrong thing or won't know what to say when they try to share their faith. Others say evangelism just is not their calling. Still others are hesitant to speak for the Lord because they fear rejection. But the Bible tells us not to fear people who can merely destroy our bodies (Matt. 10:26–28).

Develop Urgency

Oklahoma is a big wheat producing state. When the wheat ripens you can see miles and miles of sun-bleached wheat ready to be harvested. The farmers have a sense of urgency to cut their wheat and store it away safely because there is always the risk that a summer hailstorm will flatten their crop. They put most of their other work on hold as they focus their efforts on harvesting the wheat.

Jesus used a similar illustration to try to develop a sense of urgency in his disciples: "The harvest is plentiful, but the laborers are few" (Matt. 9:37). As Jesus gazed at the mass of humanity around him, he did not categorize them by their specific sins or problems. Instead, he saw them as people first—people that were distressed and needy. He likened them to sheep without a shepherd and saw them as lost sheep wandering in spiritual darkness. The Jewish leaders were not giving them the spiritual guidance they needed in order to receive salvation and eternal life in heaven. They were spiritually directionless, and without faith in God through Jesus they would be eternally lost.

How better to describe the day in which we live? People are distressed and downcast. So many are directionless, without purpose, and scared to face the future. They too are like sheep without a shepherd. Our world is filled with people who need spiritual guidance, direction, and leadership in life. Devoted disciples of Jesus should have a real sense of spiritual urgency about them. If we can live or work next to a lost person or a carnal Christian and not feel urgency about the condition of their spiritual life, there is something wrong with us.

Minister to Others

The disciples ministered to others too. They healed, comforted, and encouraged those they came in contact with. There are many ways to minister to others, but I'm thinking of one way we can be especially effective. Have you ever been able to minister to a hurting friend or family member because you had already experienced the same problem? You could support and encourage that person because you knew firsthand that someday the difficulty would end, the pain would lessen, and the faint light at the end of the tunnel would steadily grower brighter. Because of your experience and perspective, you could offer them comfort and hope.

During Marcia's first four pregnancies, the babies died either in the early weeks or in the middle of the pregnancies. Before this happened to us, Marcia and I could not comprehend all of the pain involved in such tragedies even though we tried. But afterwards, we could intimately identify with others who suffered a similar loss. Now we are able to comfort others because God led us through the same experiences as them.

Here's another example. Almost every month some pastor will call to talk to me about a struggle or pain in his life and ministry.

There was time earlier in my life when I could not have even begun to understand what they were going through. Today, though, after many years as a pastor and having gone through similar adversities, I am able to minister to them.

There is no way I would have wanted to lose those babies just so I could comfort somebody else, and I certainly would not have chosen to endure trials in my ministry just so I could comfort other pastors. But since I have endured these hardships, God has shown me the good in it. God "comforts us in all our affliction, so that we may be able to comfort those who are in any affliction, with the comfort with which we ourselves are comforted by God" (2 Cor. 1:4). It is a blessing to me to know my suffering was not wasted. Enduring a time of suffering and experiencing the power of God to see you through it gives you a passion for ministry to others like nothing else can.

Serve

Disciples serve others. Jesus said he came "not to be served but to serve" (Matt. 20:28). As the Spirit transforms our lives, we will desire to serve God by doing his will. We can exercise our spiritual gifts in the local church (1 Pet. 4:10), serving the church and others before ourselves (Gal. 5:13). Whether we are using our gifts within the body to serve one another or reaching out to the unsaved, we are worshipping God through our service. (See also Paul's discussion about how we worship God through service to others in Romans 12.)

Claim the Authority

Jesus did what he did on earth not because he was the Son of God, but because he had access to the Holy Spirit's power and authority. Once the apostles received the Holy Spirit, they were changed men. Only then did they fully understand what Christ had been teaching them and how the Holy Spirit would empower them for their mission. The same Holy Spirit who empowered Jesus and the disciples then empowers us with unquestionable spiritual authority today. The way we do ministry, whether it is through full-time vocational ministry or avocationally, is to depend upon the authority Jesus gives each of us.

Others will see he has given us the strength and authority to do the things he says that we should do. It is not just the super-Christian or the super-cleric who is supplied with spiritual authority. Every believer who spends time with Jesus receives the authority to accomplish his work.

Furthermore, the Bible tells us that God "gave the apostles, the prophets, the evangelists, the shepherds and teachers, to equip the saints for the work of ministry, for building up the body of Christ" (Eph. 4:11–12). God's plan for the New Testament church is still his plan today. It is to prepare leaders who, in turn, will equip believers for the work of service and ministry—within and without the church. The disciples (the apostles) were the men God used to train the New Testament church leaders. Today, pray that your church pastor and leaders will be godly leaders who teach and prepare those in their care for service to God.

Be Willing

Many years ago I heard God's call in my own life to full-time vocational ministry. I determined I did not have the right personality for the work, and it was not something I was willing to do. I said no to God and pursued another career path, admittedly at which I was quite successful. It took years and the pain of God's discipline before I finally came to the place where he got my attention. I repented and said, "God, I will have no god but you. If you can use me, I'm available."

I tell you with all honesty, if God can use somebody like me, he can use anybody. I can also say from experience that if your relationship with God isn't what it used to be, go back to the last time you told him no and confess it to him. Your qualification for serving is not your personality, intelligence, family background, beauty, or anything else about you except your heart. If you will turn your heart to God and determine to be passionate for following him, he will change your life and he will use you.

Some people say they want to serve God in the church—but only if they can be on the most influential committee in the church. Or only if they can serve in a place that their service will be noticed by many. Or only if they can serve with a select group of adults. These people seem never to feel called to work behind the scenes, teach children, help with the cleanup after a ministry event, or go on a construction mission trip, for example.

They are "willing" to serve on their conditions. Even though God may show them a need and place where they could serve, they do not see it as an important-enough job for them, so they say no to God. As a result, they will never be used by him.

Becoming a devoted disciple of Jesus is about living in the fellowship of his presence, learning to surrender to him, and becoming more obedient to him. As your obedience to him grows, your desire to make a difference in the world will grow.

The apostle Peter is an example of a disciple who endured to become a great servant of God. He is one of my favorite disciples, maybe because I can relate to his shortcomings and impulsiveness. Jesus prepared him and sent out to proclaim the gospel. He was transformed into a spiritual rock who accepted the mission of spreading the gospel and helping found the early church. God used him to make an unforgettable impact on the world around him. In the last years of his life, he exemplified missional living.

Before God got ahold of his heart and turned him into the man that was to be used in such powerful ways, he also struggled with idolatry and walked through some incredibly rough times. In the next chapter, we will take a closer look at his story and see how God used his four-step pattern to return Peter to intimate fellowship with him.

CHAPTER EIGHT

Peter's Pattern

Peter's world had turned upside down. Just a few short hours earlier, he and the other disciples had been in the garden with Jesus. Now he kept to the back of the crowd in the courtyard. He tried to remain invisible in the flickering shadows cast by the fire but stayed close enough to try to shake the chill that gripped him. He wanted to hear news about what was going on in these trumped-up trials. Jesus was innocent. To try him in the middle of the night was unheard of and illegal.

The shocking events of the last few hours kept playing over and over in his mind. Judas, one of his fellow disciples, had come up to their group, kissed Jesus in a usual greeting, and then everything went wrong. A mob of Jewish leaders and Roman soldiers arrested Jesus!

"Why didn't he resist them?" Peter agonized to himself. "It was almost like he willingly went with them. It wasn't supposed to end this way! And why does that servant girl keep studying me?"

He turned away to escape her scrutiny. Then someone stirred the fire. As it flared and illuminated his face, the girl's expression turned from puzzled to recognition. She confronted him.

"You're one of them. You were with Jesus."

"Woman, I don't know him."

A bit later another from the courtyard crowd repeated the accusation.

"You are too one of them."

"Man, I am not."

Fighting every instinct to flee before the crowd figured out he was lying, Peter controlled his panic and remained in the courtyard. Then one more time someone insisted he had been with Jesus.

"He was with him, for he is a Galilean too."

Cursing and swearing Peter said, "Man, I do not know what you are talking about!"

As the guards began to lead Jesus away, he turned and looked at Peter. For a second their eyes locked. Then reeling with shame and pain, Peter fled, weeping bitterly (Mark 14).

What could have possibly happened that we find Peter, the leader of the disciples and one of Jesus' closest friends, now in this state of despair?

Peter's Idols

First, a little background. While we have the joy and advantage of a post-resurrection historical point of view, Jesus' disciples did not. His disciples looked at the world through a lens of political perspective and interpreted the Old Testament Scriptures through the same lens. They believed the Scriptures predicted that the Messiah would be a powerful political ruler who would overthrow the tyrannical Roman rule and establish an earthly kingdom.

When Jesus told the disciples he would go to Jerusalem, suffer many atrocities, be killed, and be resurrected on the third day, they simply could not comprehend what he was talking about. Telling them he was going to die made no sense to them at all. It did not agree with what they "knew" was going to happen. That's why Peter responded to Jesus' predictions by reprimanding him, telling him it would never happen (Matt. 16:22). He would not accept that the Messiah they had been waiting for all these years would be killed, nor could he understand that he would be resurrected. Peter wanted a powerful, earthly leader, and nothing else would do.

Then it was Jesus' turn to rebuke Peter. "Get behind me, Satan! You are a hindrance to me. For you are not setting your mind on the things of God, but on the things of man" (Matt. 16:23). Ouch! That had to sting. How would we feel if we were Peter? He was one of the inner circle of disciples and a close friend to Jesus. Yet Jesus scolded him and called him a hindrance in front of everyone. How humiliating.

Hmmm. Personal desires instead of godly desires? Self-interest instead of God's interests? This had better sound familiar to us by now and set off warnings. Peter's personal desires became his idols. It happens so easily.

Have you ever made a purchase or a decision and then later prayed that God would bless it? I remember buying a car one time, and after I bought it I prayed to God and said something like, "Now, I know you're for this, right? I'm going to use it in your work. Please bless my decision." It was a little bit late to ask his blessing. I had already made the purchase based solely on my desire.

Or I've heard some people say, "Well, I know the Bible says I should only marry a believer, but I'm positive God has sent this person to me. Even though he's not a Christian, I just know I can bring him to Christ, so it's really okay that I want to marry him." Again, it is a backward situation. Asking what God's will is should have taken place before ever beginning the relationship.

Let's back up to a little earlier in the evening and look in on Jesus' final Passover meal with his disciples. "You will all fall away because of me this night. For it is written, 'I will strike the shepherd, and the sheep of the flock will be scattered,' " Jesus said (Matt. 26:31). But always the arrogant, self-confident one, Peter bragged that though everyone else might betray Jesus, he would never deny him. Jesus challenged his boast, saying not only would he deny him, but that he would do it that very night. And not just once but three times.

Peter's brash actions were symptomatic of another idol: self-determination.

We can relate. When life is really tough and our backs are up against the wall, do we rely on our own strength or the Lord's to solve the problem? Who do we turn to first? Ourselves? Friends? God—only as our last resort? We know we ought to trust, obey, and take what he says as the truth, but instead we try to use our fleshly self-determination to get what we want. For example, we tap our intellectual ability or personality. Or we rely on our education, strength, or relationship with someone. Daily we're tempted to depend on our own determination or self-control instead of depending on and trusting the Lord.

As a pastor, I preach a lot of sermons. I can do my best to make sure that the exegesis of the passage is correct. The delivery could be flawless, hypothetically speaking, of course. All of the sermon points could start with the same letter, which makes it nice and tidy and easy to remember when that happens. What I say could be one-hundred-percent true, but if the words of the sermon have come only from my mind, my education, my personal research, and from my efforts, then what I deliver to my congregation is hollow. In order for me to deliver life to the audience through a sermon, the Holy Spirit has to have created it in me.

When Peter denied Jesus three times in the courtyard, yet another idol of Peter's was revealed: self-protection. We might be thinking, "It's natural to protect yourself. Give Peter a break. What more would God want than that?" I think God would want us to allow him to protect us rather than us relying on self-protection.

How often does God try to warn and protect us, but we don't see it? Jesus had predicted Peter would deny him. He had also given Peter the opportunity to pray in the garden earlier in the evening to fortify his spirit, but instead Peter slept. These were both warnings—ignored warnings.

Peter did not make another man his god. He did not make his career, money, or material possessions his god. Nor did he turn his religion into his god. Instead, Peter bowed to his desires and abilities: self-determination, self-control, and self-protection.

Peter's Wake-Up Call

Convicted of his sin, Peter must have felt as if a thousand-pound weight had crashed down on him. Immediately after his third denial and the rooster crowed the second time, Peter remembered Jesus' earlier prophecy—the early warning sign he had ignored. But now God had his full attention, that first step in the pattern of God calling us back to him. The arrogant apostle had trusted himself and failed horribly. He burned with shame for what he had done.

One of the things I love about Peter, though, is that he did not try to justify what he did, and he did not try to rationalize it. Instead, we're told he wept bitterly. He was deeply sorrowful for his actions. It was the beginning of his repentance. "Be wretched and mourn and weep. Let your laughter be turned to mourning and your joy to gloom" (James 4:9). One commentator sums up the gist of this passage this way: "Recognition of the tremendous need for cleansing allows no room for merriment."[1]

Revelation

Of course, we know what happens to Jesus. He was crucified and buried. Then on the third day after his death, some women and disciples went to the tomb. An angel spoke to them, saying, "He is not here. See the place where they laid him. But go, tell his disciples *and Peter*" (Mark 16:6–7, emphasis added).

How would Peter have felt when these folks returned to the house and excitedly proclaimed that Jesus was resurrected from the dead? Incredulous excitement. And probably also apprehension, thinking about his betrayal of his Master. When they told Peter the angel at the tomb specifically mentioned him among those that Jesus wanted to meet with, a wave of relief must have washed over him. Jesus issued a specific invitation to Peter to come meet with him. He still wanted to see him even after his three-time denial. Jesus issues the same invitation of fellowship to us.

After hearing that Jesus was gone from the tomb, Peter immediately ran to see for himself. He marveled at what had happened. Finally he was beginning to "get it."

Jesus met with his disciples after his resurrection, and although we are not told everything he said in his meeting with them, Mark tells us he rebuked them for their lack of faith (16:14). It was imperative for the disciples to understand the implications of him being the *risen* Savior who had power over death. Now because of this demonstration of his divineness and further revelation of his holiness, the disciples' sin of doubt and personal aspirations became crystal clear to them. The lens through which they had judged Jesus' mission as a political one was now shattered. For the first time perhaps, Jesus' true, heavenly mission began to come into focus.

Confession and Repentance

Remember, Jesus was crucified before Peter's relationship with him could be restored. By the time the disciples and Peter met with Jesus, Peter was feeling full-fledged repentance for his shameful denials and the idols he had put above his Lord. If we could have eavesdropped on the conversation between them, we most likely would have heard Peter confessing over and over again how sorry and ashamed he was, seeking Jesus' forgiveness. Repentance, the third step in God's pattern for calling our hearts back to him, provides the path toward a fresh, new beginning and restored, wonderful intimacy with Jesus.

If you have been following some substitute god of your own creation, repent and return to God. If there have been times when your testimony was weak and you felt the shame of not speaking up for Jesus, confess it. Restoration comes through conviction and repentance.

Transformation and Mission

During the forty days after Jesus' resurrection the Bible only gives us glimpses of Peter. The next close look at him is in Acts 2 when Peter preached a sermon in Jerusalem on the day of Pentecost. What a remarkable turnaround. Is this the same man? Now he is boldly preaching the gospel message. His transformation from a coward who denied Christ before a lowly servant girl to a confident apostle preaching to several thousand people is evidence of God's transforming work. His preaching was so powerful that three thousand people were saved at the conclusion of his message.

What was his mission? The fourth and final step? To grow more deeply as a devoted disciple and engage in service to God by telling others about the saving grace of Jesus Christ.

Isaiah and Peter: Similarities and Contrasts

There are many similarities between Peter's and Isaiah's experiences. First, both had let idols lure their hearts away from God. One idolized a man instead of God; one idolized his self-interests.

Next, each experienced a crisis to get his attention. Isaiah lost his hero and along with him lost the security and continuity everyone in the nation enjoyed under him. Peter believed he was losing Jesus and the dreams of political power. His Messiah was on trial; conviction and crucifixion seemed certain. But his real wake-up call was the penetrating look from his Lord after three, self-serving denials.

The revelations to each were quite different. Isaiah's vision of the magnificent scene in the heavenly throne room was nothing like the revelation to Peter that began at the empty stone tomb. The result was the same, however. Both men responded with repentance.

And finally, both dedicated their lives to serving the Lord. For Isaiah, the future held a preaching ministry that would be amazingly important and surprisingly unpopular. Peter would go on to be a preacher, missionary, elder, and human author of New Testament epistles. Later, tradition tells us, he would be crucified upside down, insisting he was unworthy to be crucified in the exact manner his Lord and Savior was.[2]

What Does It Mean for Us?

Sometimes God will grab our attention through spectacular events—huge defining moments that shake us to our core. This might happen during a crisis such as the loss of a loved one, catastrophic illness, or personal tragedy. At other times, God will call softly and gently to us through his written Word and much more subtle events. The pattern is not always clear-cut, but I have seen it played out many times in the lives of believers.

Remain vigilant and watchful. Whether it is a monumentally defining moment or one sentence in the Bible speaking directly to us, we should view such experiences as one-way street signs turning us back to intimacy with Christ.

I suspect many of us identify with the sometimes brash, impulsive, blundering, and yet sincere apostle. We tend to snicker at some of the quick and poor decisions Peter made such as cutting off the ear of the high priest's servant (John 18:10). And we shake our heads at his boastful declaration that all of the rest of the apostles might betray Christ, but he would never do such a thing. But there is some of this man in all of us.

The change in Peter's heart affected great change in the lives of countless others. Hopefully, we will be willing to let the same Spirit who filled Peter and allowed him to become a bold proclaimer of Christ fill and equip us for our mission too.

CHAPTER NINE

Changed Hearts; Changed Nation

There are those who believe our nation has gone too far away from God for too long and that there is no hope for America. They must have a very poor understanding of history, however, and certainly they must have a poor understanding of God's power. History and the Bible both tell us that the direction of a nation can be changed.

Spiritual change follows a rather simple process. First, it starts in the hearts of individuals, then it spreads to the church, and only then can it be realized in the nation. God calls us—individuals and churches—to repent and return to him so he can use us to prepare the way for his great work among the unsaved.

The Old Testament prophets often began their prophecies by saying something like, "The Lord is about a great work. He is coming with might and power upon his people." Then they would call for the people to repent of sins and turn to God. The prophets of today are the preachers in our pulpits, but the message is the same: before God changes the course of a nation or city, the church and the people in it have to be going in the right direction. When we repent and turn our hearts fully to Christ and our lampstands burn bright and strong, then get ready to watch God work. Some would say we need to get ready for revival.

Historical Revival and Reformation

Most of us don't study church history, which is our loss because it can reveal a panoramic view of the way God works. Those who study it will learn that there have been appallingly dangerous times when the church was defiled and diluted by the society of that era. Those were dark days in the history of our world. But on the other hand, there have also been miraculous times when God intervened, reviving and restoring the church.

By the sixteenth century, the church had become thoroughly corrupt. Liturgical religion ruled. Traditionalism was more important than the Bible, and formality and ritual religion were the order of the day. But then God moved. He began by speaking to one man—Martin Luther. God gifted him with great insight into the spiritual truths of the Bible. The result? The Protestant Reformation.

During this time God rekindled a hunger for his Word among believers. They also restored Scripture to a place of authority and influence. It ignited a revival of the church. Luther is a wonderful example of God using one willing servant to impact great change.

Something similar occurred in American history in the 1700s. The church was at a very low point, and immorality was rampant in this nation. Sometimes we think those early days of our colonial ancestors were godly, moral, and puritanical. But the 1730s was a time of gross immorality. There was terrible ignorance of the Bible and widespread rebellion against God.

Then God sent men such as George Whitefield, Gilbert Tennent, and Jonathan Edwards to preach to our nation. They preached about a holy God and the need to be right with a holy God. Revival began to shake and shape the nation. It became known as the First

Great Awakening.[1] Out of that time of restoring of God's Word and the resulting revival among God's people, the Declaration of Independence was born. The United States is a nation that was born in the middle of a revival. Now we are a nation that needs to be *reborn* in the middle of a revival.

What just came to your mind when I said "revival"? A weeklong series of special services at a church with an evangelist? An evangelistic crusade, held in coliseum or giant performance hall? I'm not talking about those. Revival is an often misunderstood and misapplied term.

Revival refers to a spiritual awakening. It's a time when God reveals himself to his people and they renew their commitment to him, deepening their relationship. It may be more than that but never less. It's when what we believe about God takes root in our lives and changes the way we act. Revival happens when believers accept God's authority and submit to him in obedience. It is really nothing other than a return to New Testament Christianity and restoration of authority to God's Word.

A little over a century ago, Wales experienced the 1904 national religious revival. It began in a youth meeting and grew over the next year to become a revival that ultimately saw over one hundred thousand people accept Jesus. It all began because God prepared a young man, Evan Roberts, so he could prepare the way for him. From that one man, God spread the fires of spiritual renewal to the church and then throughout the entire nation.[2]

Luther and Evans are examples of how God initiated great change starting with one man. Now let's look at Josiah, who impacted great change in his nation.

One Man Influencing Change in a Nation

The nation was in decline socially, militarily, and economically. Tragically, the people had pursued tolerance to the exclusion of truth. Immorality had become an accepted lifestyle. The people lived for themselves, and they lived for the moment. They had abandoned the God of their forefathers and turned to foreign gods. Some future historian could easily write those words about the day in which we live, but these words were written to describe the nation of Judah in 622 BC.

Judah was a nation of God's chosen people, but in no way did it resemble a godly nation at that time. Then one man, Josiah, decided he would live for the Lord. He committed to live every day of his life as God's man, in God's way, doing what God wanted him to do. He also happened to be the king of this great, but now spiritually bereft, nation.

Josiah's life was an about-face to that of his predecessors. Both his grandfather and father were evil, godless kings who led the people of Judah into idol worship. His grandfather ruled fifty-five years, but God's patience with their evil ways must have reached the limit with Josiah's father because after only two years he removed him from power by having his own servants kill him. So at the young age of eight years, Josiah inherited the throne and ruled for thirty-one years.

At some point, Josiah was convicted to restore corporate worship of God among the people. (He's a good example of how we don't have to become a bad product of our environment and personal history.) First, he dedicated himself to restoring the temple, which had long remained unused for its intended purpose. It was in shameful disrepair. Some biblical experts think it was being used as a type of warehouse for unused items. It seems inconceivable that the temple, where God had met with his people and his people had worshipped him, could be relegated to a dilapidated storehouse of forgotten items. It had even been used for worship of pagan gods.

As workmen began the restoration, they uncovered an important-looking book, and they took it to the scribe. As the scribe examined it and began to read from it, he immediately recognized the content. It was the Book of Law. He had not seen it for many, many years. Believe it or not, the people of Judah had lost the Bible. Ironically, they had lost the Bible in the church. Somewhere along the line, people began to follow philosophy, or perhaps politics and economics, more than they desired to follow God. Sooner or later, they heard less and less about God's Word until, finally, it was just put on a shelf and buried under debris.

The scribe took the old book to King Josiah and read it to him. It was the first time in his life he had heard God's Word, and it revealed a sharp contrast between the way he was living and the way God intended. Now convicted of his disobedience and sin, he repented. The Lord said, "Because your heart was penitent, and you humbled yourself before the Lord…and wept before me, I also have heard you" (2 Kings 22:19).

Josiah experienced personal revival, but he didn't want to keep it to himself. He wanted the people of his country to experience it. First, he ordered the pagan idols destroyed. Then everything pertaining to Baal and Asherah worship was removed from the temple, burned, and the ashes carried far away. He also "deposed the priests…who burned incense to Baal, to the sun and the moon and the constellations and all the host of the heavens" (2 Kings 23:5).

Josiah is remembered as a remarkable king who restored a declining nation. But more importantly, he led the spiritual reformation of the nation. God brought a dramatic change to Judah when one man had a change of heart and decided to do right in the sight of the Lord and walk in the ways of David.

Reform of Today's Church

Josiah saw a need to restore and repair the church in his day. What about the church today? Sadly, there may be an even greater need to repair today's churches. Not the buildings but the church—the people and leaders who fill those buildings and pulpits. Throughout history corruption has occurred within the church, and today it continues to occur at an alarming rate. It is not just the heretical church, or the cultic church, or the bizarre, fringe church that needs to be repaired. Even many conservative, Bible-believing, evangelical churches need an overhaul of their value system. The church is not what it needs to be in our country today. It is in disarray.

Unfortunately, today many Christians and churches have exchanged a driving desire for a heaven-sent revival for a desire for a moral environment of convenience for themselves. They want a moral nation in which to raise their children, to live their own lives in peace, and to do their work productively. There is nothing wrong with those things, but they are achieving something quite different. They have settled for something other than God's best.

Some Christians feel helpless to change the direction of the country. Thinking that nothing they do will make any difference, they sit idly by. Others stake too much on changing the nation through political means, working tirelessly to achieve political victories. Their rhetoric is about restoring conservative values when instead they need to be talking about evangelism, discipleship, and submission to Christ. Even good Bible-believing churches can be caught up in seeking political solutions rather than spiritual solutions to the problems that face us.

I'm sometimes criticized because I don't speak out about political issues. It's not because I am not concerned about who our leaders should be or the state of our country. I am. It's not because I don't care about the social issues and the moral state of our country. I do. But I am called to preach the Word of God to change people's hearts, and I believe people with changed hearts who put God first will do the right thing for themselves, their neighbors, and their nation.

There is one hope for the future. One hope for your family. One hope for your church. One hope for this nation. That hope is not in party politics, political action groups, elections, marches, or crusades. Instead, our hope is in a reformation among God's people so that the Bible will be restored to a place of authority. When it permeates our lives and our families' lives and becomes the standard by which we live, the nation has a chance to experience revival.

Before revival can happen in the nation, though, churches and the people in them need to examine themselves. At the basic core of the church's problems are disobedience and idolatry in the form of desires for community recognition, popularity, numerical growth, denominational status, and other self-centered pursuits over their desire for God. For example, in many churches form has replaced substance; entertainment has replaced worship and ministry; desire for increased numbers has replaced theology and truth; traditionalism has replaced the Bible; and ritual religion and relativism have replaced God in many gatherings that have the word church above the door.

Furthermore, churches have become astonishingly tolerant of errant preaching and teaching, immorality, and spiritual childishness among their members. Some popular Christian leaders seem to take great pride in "rewriting" the Bible for their own convenience and then teaching their congregations their own unique interpretations. This is heresy and false teaching. How sad because they will have to stand accountable before God one day.

In many churches, ministries and worship have flip-flopped from God-centered to man-centered. They have turned sermons into positive-thinking seminars and the church into therapeutic treatment centers. Songs, prayers, and sermons focus on making members feel good and helping them achieve success in this earthly life rather than focusing on the person and glory of God.

Churches have to move beyond personal opinions and traditions and instead measure everything they do against God's Word, seeking the Holy Spirit's help to conform fully to God's will and way. When we Christians come to the place of not just fighting about the inerrancy and infallibility of the Bible but actually believing and becoming expert students of it, then we can apply it in our personal lives, families, churches, and nation. Christians who have experienced repentance, repaired lives, and revival will make strong churches. In turn, strong churches can spiritually revive a nation.

Living Expectantly

I was not expecting revival when I preached to the Silver Cliff students. Even though I sensed God was directing my sermon topic down a different path, I never anticipated just how significantly he would work in the lives of those students. I thought the sermon I preached on idolatry was very ordinary, but God chose to use it to produce extraordinary results. The lesson for me was that I should live more expectantly of what his mighty power can do in our lives.

What our students experienced that summer at Silver Cliff was not left on a Colorado mountainside. That unusual movement of the Holy Spirit returned with us to our church. He worked in our congregation in amazing ways.

Oftentimes what he was calling us to do wasn't easy. Sometimes God called us to step way beyond our comfort zone in our obedience to him. That was the case for one of our pastors a few months after the stewardship banquet.

One evening during a staff retreat, this pastor came to me in tears. "God has put on my heart that there's something I need to do, and he wants me to do it now," he said. He then shared this passage in James: "Is anyone among you sick? Let him call for the elders of the church, and let them pray over him, anointing him with oil in the name of the Lord. And the prayer of faith will save the one who is sick" (James 5:14–15).

You see, his wife had been struggling with an amoeba in her eyes, and it had done great damage already. The damage was so extensive that she was unable to see out of one eye, and her other eye was becoming progressively worse. The prognosis was dire. Without a quick turnaround, she probably would lose her sight in both eyes.

"God has been telling me to do what it says to do in this passage, and I haven't done it. Will you do this?" he asked. It wasn't easy for this pastor and his wife to come to me with this request. It was something out of the ordinary that we pastors and elders had not done before. But the next Sunday morning after the worship service, we gathered around his wife to pray and did just what the James passage instructed.

This was not a "healing line" or the kind of sensationalism used in some churches today, which is absolutely not biblical. But if we are going to have no gods but God, we will be obedient to what his Word says. We simply tried to obey.

The next day, he and his wife called me and asked if they could stop by my office. A short while later, through tears of relief and joy, they exuberantly shared about the miraculous blessing they had just received. After the neuro-ophthalmologist, who was also a member and elder of our church, had examined her eyes this time, he declared that nothing short of a miracle had to have occurred. Her eyes were now corrected to 20/15 in both eyes, and the amoeba was gone. We rejoiced together. This miracle was yet another confirmation of God's extraordinary work among us.

As Christians, we should live expectantly. We should expect God to show up in our lives and in our church. Does he still reveal his presence to us today? I believe so. It may rarely be like in the miracle I just described. But he teaches us through his Word, convicts us of sin, and grants joy in the midst of loss. He gives insight into his presence through creation and demonstrates expressions of grace to us at just the right time and place. He changes people's lives through redemptive acts. These are all ways he reveals his work and presence to us.

Sometimes God's revelation is a personal, one-on-one encounter. But sometimes it's in a more widespread, rather public way too. For example, he revealed his presence to us in a special way during corporate gatherings at Silver Cliff and again at the stewardship banquet. Throughout the Bible we'll find a repeating pattern of God speaking to people, calling them, and sending them out. God typically reveals himself mightily to the few before he reveals himself to the crowd. But he can and does reveal himself to the masses.

The message of the Luke 12 passage (be alert for the signs) applies to us today. We need to keep our eyes open and look for ways God is working all around us. We need to be sensitive to his ways. Then his work will become more and more apparent to us.

"Have no gods but God" and "Get ready!" was God's two-part message to our church at the stewardship banquet. "Get ready" no doubt means we're to prepare as I've earlier described a disciple of Christ preparing for service. But it has another application for us too—to get ready for what can happen when we turn away from idols and return our hearts to God. When we have no gods but God, we will see our great and mighty God move in powerful ways. Expect great things to happen. Get ready for revival!

I believe we live in a day in which revival is beginning to occur. We are witnessing an outpouring of God's Spirit—life-changing encounters with the Spirit of God—in this nation. Some people might argue that the United States is heading more quickly to hell than to revival, but there are signs pointing to mighty changes in the future. For example, there is a renewed commitment to biblical theology. Young pastors seem truly dedicated to the spiritual growth of members rather than simply enlarging church membership. And many young people are sold out to living for Christ.

God is sending revival—not some hyper-emotional evangelistic crusade but a display of his power and will among and through his people. He is bringing revival unlike anything I've ever seen in the ministry.

The Opportunity

We live in strange times. The economy is stressed, there are cultural changes happening around the world, and terrorism is a constant threat. Job insecurity and fear for the future are commonplace. Peace between nations seems more elusive than ever, and even nature seems to be in rebellion. It's not that these things haven't happened before; they have. But there is a convergence of these forces and an intensification of their severity that seems unique. Maybe it is an indication of something special to come.

Wouldn't it be something if God came in such a way to this nation that television programming, movies and other amusements, and certain medical, ethical, and moral issues were revolutionized without seeking a political force but because of the Holy Spirit's power?

And wouldn't it be something if God came to your city and your state and in such a mighty way that believers lived lives fully devoted to him, thousands of our neighbors came to Christ, and people were drawn here from all over the world just to see what God was doing?

Perhaps there has not been another time exactly like this since the 1700s when a country was born in the middle of a revival. We live in a time we cannot take lightly. Opportunities like this are rare indeed. Imagine what that means to you. God has allowed you to be alive at a moment in time when his Spirit is being poured out in a nation to turn that nation back to him. God is giving us the understanding of responsibility to do as Josiah did and not waiver to the left or to the right but to walk in all the ways of our forefathers.

Are you starting to sense God dealing with you about this now? I would simply say to you, "Let God be God, and get ready."

CHAPTER TEN

Final Thoughts

The words in this book chronicle God's ongoing work in the lives of his people. For many years, he has taught the body at Henderson Hills Baptist Church what it means to have no gods but God. He is continually wooing us back to himself, following the pattern I have outlined. The simple truth of these lessons continues to have a profound impact on our lives as we seek to improve our relationship with him and with each other and enjoy the reward of intimate fellowship with our Lord. We continue to learn, make mistakes, struggle, repent, and renew our commitment to have no gods but God and to prepare ourselves for what God will do.

Imagine a group of Christians who have matured in their walk with Christ to the point that many of the doubts and questions they once had have been answered. These are people who demonstrate remarkable love for others, joy about the Lord's presence and work in their lives, and peace in the midst of trying circumstances. They have found satisfaction in their relationship with God.

Of course, they still make mistakes, but many of the sins that used to haunt them have been put aside. The people of their church depend on this group of believers. They have a level of fellowship with Christ and a wisdom that makes them remarkably valuable to others. The church is blessed by these Christians because they take responsibility for others, play a vital role in leading the lost to Christ, and disciple new believers.

Now, imagine that you are a member of that group. In fact, that is God's will for you. I pray that through this account you too have learned lessons to help you experience God in a deeper, more intimate way.

❧❧

The Bowery Mission

Does the name Victor Benke mean anything to you? Probably not, and it didn't to me either until several years ago. I heard it for the first time when my wife's parents were shaking their family tree. Marcia's mother's grandfather was named Victor Benke, and he, as the story goes, was an Austrian immigrant who migrated to the United States around the turn of the twentieth century. He was purported to be an organist of some renown who had an impact on the Bowery Mission in New York City and who also wrote a number of hymns. The whole story didn't mean much to me at first.

Then a few years ago Marcia and I were in New York while I was teaching a short course at Nyack College and Alliance Theological Seminary. The schools treated us to a couple extra days in New York, so we went to a Broadway show and explored the city. Marcia mentioned her desire to locate the Bowery Mission, and we set out to climb the family tree.

After a long subway ride, a story in itself, we finally got off on Spring Street and walked west to Bowery. We made our way north a couple of blocks, past the graffiti and Chinese restaurants, to the only red brick building with signage identifying it as the Bowery Mission.

We entered the building and carefully worked our way through a number of homeless men who were sitting in the lobby. If the walls of this old building could talk, I'm sure they would have amazing stories to tell. Constructed in the 1870s, I imagine immigrants from Ireland, Germany, Poland, and many other European countries that were coming to America in search of opportunity passed through these doors in search of food and shelter. Few would have had resources, so often they were left on the streets to fend for themselves. Many ended up at the Bowery Mission.

Decades passed, the faces changed, but the stories remained remarkably the same—tales of shattered dreams, addiction, lost hope, hard times, empty stomachs, loneliness, and hurt. Men found their way to the Bowery Mission, needing food, clothing, shelter, understanding, and most of all, the gospel. They came during World War I, and then during the Great Depression their numbers increased dramatically. World War II, Korea, and Viet Nam contributed more. There were years of prosperity but more years of scarcity. Their stories were different in some ways but the same in others—they were men who needed help and Jesus.

That's what we saw when we entered the doors of that old mission in the lower eastside of New York City one cold afternoon in November. The door swung open and we walked to a reception counter. A man greeted us with a warm smile. He could see we didn't quite fit the description of their regular visitors, and Marcia explained that her great-grandfather, Victor Benke, had played the organ there many years ago, according to family legend.

"Victor Benke," the man said, "I think I know that name." Our hearts quickened as we responded with surprise that someone outside of the family knew the name. Then it came to him. In a flash he spun on his heels, motioned, and led us into the old chapel. We followed, not knowing what to expect. There, positioned on the wall, greeting us at the entrance into the chapel was a plaque. Our host pointed to it and said, " 'Victor Benke.' I knew that I had seen that name." Tears began to roll down Marcia's face as she read the words. It read,

> *In loving memory of Victor H. Benke*
> *"The Volunteer Organist"*
> *Born in Austria 1873—Converted in this Mission*
> *1894—Called Home July 15, 1904*
> *For Ten Years He Was the Organist of the Bowery*
> *Mission and His Rare Musical Gifts Drew Many to*
> *Christ. The Men of the Bowery Loved Him.*
> *"They that turn many to righteousness shall*
> *shine as the stars forever and ever."*

It was a special moment. After reading those words several times, we walked through the rows of old pews, stared at the ancient pipes that been attached to Benke's pipe organ, and read the verses emblazoned on the walls. Our hearts ached for the homeless men that still adorned areas of the room. One man had both legs amputated. Another sat asleep in a wheelchair. Still other men sat in groups of two and three talking in hushed tones.

How many men have occupied these pews, heard the gospel, and received care, food, and protection? Another question, the most important question of all, is how many men are in heaven today because of the ministry provided at this mission by Christians through the years? There is little doubt the numbers would swell into the thousands.

Benke turned out not only to be a volunteer organist but also a hymn writer, close friend of the famous songwriter Fannie Crosby, and organist for D. L. Moody. On December 3, 1899, the *New York Times* ran an article titled, "A TRAMP, NOW ORGANIST. Bowery Mission Hears Victor Benke's Story, Rejoicing with Him at His Conversion Anniversary." Imagine. A homeless immigrant, surviving through the generosity of a rescue mission, had been transformed into a renowned organist, composer, and friend of one of the most famous men of his day.

I wonder what Mr. Moody thought of Victor Benke. Although we won't know until we see him in heaven, a sermon preached by Dr. R. A. Torrey in 1923 may give us some idea. Torrey was a Christian apologist, pastor, evangelist, author, and composer. In his sermon Torrey quoted Mr. Moody as having said, "It remains to be seen what God will do with a man who gives himself up wholly to Him."[1] I would like to think that Moody watched Victor Benke and knew that he was an illustration of what happens when a man has no gods but God.

The question I leave you with is, what will be said of your life? It's not about how much you accomplish in life for God. God does not need to have your help. It's not about how successful you are and who you know. What matters is having an intimate relationship with God. Don't just keep going through life content with the status quo of an unfulfilling Christian life. There is so much more.

Will you be a person who has no gods but God? If so, yours will be a life well spent.

Appendix

How Can I Have a Relationship with Jesus Christ?

Most of us dread the thought of offending somebody—especially when that somebody has any kind of authority over us. Laughing at a police officer is usually, and appropriately, judged a bad idea. When we were kids, causing trouble in school when the principal was watching was not a good idea—unless we wanted to suffer the consequences. Talking back to our boss (or our parents) is not good idea. Offending those in positions of authority over us is something we should naturally not want to do.

And yet that's exactly what the Bible tells us that we humans are all guilty of doing. Widespread, universal insubordination. But the authority we've offended is not just a parent, a boss, or a police officer. We've managed to offend the absolute last being in the entire cosmos that we should ever want to offend—God.

The Bible tells us that all of us are sinners (Rom. 3:23). Sin isn't some sort of impersonal "slip-up," as we tend to think of it—something that's perhaps unfortunate for all but usually unintentional and always forgivable. Sin is presented in the Bible as a personal affront to God. We've neglected to worship him, instead giving our attention and affections to other non-God things and persons, including ourselves. We've spurned his ways and chosen to make our own paths. We live like we know better than God—like we are God.

Sin is high treason against the King of the Universe. We've offended God. And he's angry about it.

Fortunately, that's not the end of the story. While there's nothing that we could ever do to mend the hostile divine-human relationship, the Bible tells us that God has done what only he could do. He has given his Son, Jesus, who came into this world and took on human flesh. And this Son of God who has eternally existed even before the creation of the universe (Col. 1:16–17) not only lived as a man but suffered as a man and finally died as a man on a cross.

Why? For what reason? The Bible leaves no mystery as to why Jesus lived the life he lived and died the death he died. Jesus didn't die because of any wrong he had committed. He was sinless. He died because of the wrongs that others had done. He died to save sinners.

The Son of God suffered God's holy wrath, which was stored up for sinners, so that they wouldn't have to. Jesus became our substitute, dying in our place so that we might live and suffering God's wrath in our place so that we might know God's peace and forgiveness. "[God the Father] made him who knew no sin [God the Son, Jesus], to be sin so that in him we might become the righteousness of God" (2 Cor. 5:21).

At the cross, God the Father poured out his wrath on God the Son, as if Jesus was sin itself, so that we might be treated and judged by the Father as Christ really was—righteous and sinless.

What's more, three days after dying Jesus got up from his own grave, proving his own deity and proving the victory now accomplished over death. The Father accepted the Son's sacrifice for sinners, and so he raised him from the grave.

This is unimaginably good news. What a twist of plot, turning an awful story into an amazingly wonderful story. But there's still another piece to be added to this gospel puzzle, and it is a critical one. Jesus' death on the cross doesn't simply wipe clean the sins of everybody in the history of the world so that now everybody has a clean slate and a fresh start with God. Rather, it calls for a specific response, apart from which nobody will ever be saved.

That response is two-fold: repentance and faith. Repentance is turning away from the way of sinners. Away from worshipping things, persons, or ourselves. Away from following the ways of this world and following our own rules. And faith is turning toward God, who through Christ has made this possible. Toward worshipping him and him alone. Toward submitting now to him, following his commands and his ways.

These are two sides to the same coin. You can't have one without the other. And you can't have salvation without either. Jesus stands as a substitute, bearing wrath and judgment and bringing peace and reconciliation to all who "repent and believe [i.e., have faith] in the gospel" (Mark 1:15).

Lastly, let me offer a few practical suggestions for those of you contemplating this gospel message. Maybe you're convinced and ready for action, or maybe you're skeptical of this message but would like to learn more. Wherever you are, let me offer a few last, vital words.

First, devote yourself to studying the Bible and to prayer. The Bible is God's authoritative revelation, given to man as a gift so that man might know God and know how to be reconciled to him. As you read, submit yourself to what you learn, and then pray to God in light of what you've read.

Second, God doesn't save individuals who are to then tough

it out on their own. Although salvation is a call to a one-on-one relationship with God, he also calls us into a community. That community, which Jesus himself founded (Matt. 16:18), is called the Church. And that Church, made up of all Christians of all time, consists of local expressions across the world—local churches. Find a local church that believes and teaches this gospel message, and commit yourself to that body of believers. The local church is God's greenhouse for the Christian to grow and mature in.

And then lastly, a warning that I hope you will find encouraging: Coming to God through Christ (becoming a Christian) doesn't mean that you will then, magically, cease from sinning. It does mean, however, that God gives you his Holy Spirit. It does mean that we don't have to sin anymore. We're no longer dead and helpless in our sins, but we've been made alive by God's Spirit (Eph. 2:5)—alive to battle and to choose God instead of sin. Christians fail and fall, but they get back up and they battle by God's grace. And their failures aren't counted against them; they've been counted against Jesus who has suffered and died in their place.

If you've never repented of your sins, confessed him as your Lord, and accepted his invitation to have a personal relationship with him, I urge you to do so right now.

Notes

CHAPTER TWO

1. Herbert Schlossberg, *Idols for Destruction—The Conflict of Christian Faith and American Culture* (Wheaton, IL: Crossway, 1990), 6.
2. Timothy Keller, *Counterfeit Gods, The Empty Promises of Money, Sex, and Power, and the Only Hope that Matters* (New York: Dutton, 2009), xvii-xix.
3. Richard Keyes, "The Idol Factory." In *No God But God*, eds. Os Guinness and John Seel (Chicago, IL: Moody Press, 1992), 33.
4. Ibid. 39.
5. Keller, *Counterfeit Gods*, 66.
6. John Calvin, *Institutes of the Christian Religion* (Bellingham, WA: Logos Research Systems, Inc., 1997), I.XI.8.
7. Keyes, *No God But God*, 37.
8. *The Pulpit Commentary: Proverbs.* Ed. H. D. M. Spence-Jones (Bellingham, WA: Logos Research Systems, Inc.,2004), 413.
9. A letter from Luther to Duke George of Saxony.
10. Keller, *Counterfeit Gods*, 23.
11. Charles Rollin, *The Ancient History of the Egyptians, Carthaginians, Assyrians, Babylonians, Medes and Persians, Macedonians and Grecians*, 6 vols., (New York: George Dearborn, 1836), 2:193.

CHAPTER THREE

1. Guinness and Seel, *No God But God*, 24.
2. James Dobson, *The New Dare to Discipline* (Wheaton, IL: Tyndale House, 1992), 7.

3. "Forty million years" was Borglum's statement. I am not commenting on the age of the earth. That is a different discussion for a different study.

4. Henry T. Blackaby and Claude V. King, *Fresh Encounter* (Nashville, TN: Lifeway Press, 1993), 64.

5. Ibid., 62.

6. Wayne Grudem, *Systematic Theology, An Introduction to Biblical Doctrine* (Grand Rapids, MI: Zondervan, 1994), 505-6.

7. John F. Walvoord, Roy B. Zuck and Dallas Theological Seminary, *The Bible Knowledge Commentary: An Exposition of the Scriptures*, Re 2:1 (Wheaton, IL: Victor Books, 1983).

8. Jesus was very clear on the responsibilities of church discipline (Matt. 18:15–17), and it is clearly addressed in many other places in the New Testament, too. The apostle Paul speaks of this kind of discipline (Rom. 16:17, 1 Cor. 5:9–13, Gal. 6:1, 1 Tim. 1:19–20, and Titus 3:10). Likewise, the apostle John mentions it (3 John 9–10). The church in Thyatira, mentioned in Revelation, tolerated sin among its members and received a significant rebuke from the Lord (2:18–29). If a member is divisive to church unity, the Lord desires for this discipline to occur. If a Christian becomes morally or ethically disobedient to Christ, then that member is to be disciplined. Additionally, the teaching of false doctrine is a very specific occasion by which the Lord will discipline a Christian through his church (Titus 1:9–11; 3:10; Acts 20:27).

9. Robert C. Loveless, "Every Day with Jesus," © 1936 – Percy B. Crawford.

CHAPTER FOUR

1. Schlossberg, *Idols for Destruction*, 39.
2. Guinness and Seel, *No God But God*, 161.

³ R. Stanton Norman, "Human Sinfulness." In *A Theology for the Church*, ed. Daniel L. Akin, (Nashville: B&H Academic, 2007) 430.
⁴ Grudem, *Systematic Theology*, 490.

CHAPTER FIVE

¹ Kenneth D. Ackerman, *Dark Horse* (New York: Carroll & Graff Publishers, 2003), 383-440.

CHAPTER SIX

¹ Robert Murray McCheyne, minister in the Church of Scotland from 1835 to 1843.

CHAPTER SEVEN

¹ The verse says that God asked, "Who will go for us?" Notice the plural. The "us" is the Trinity. God is saying, "Who will go for me, the Father? Who will go for me, the Son? Who goes for me, the Holy Spirit?" When we deal with God, we shouldn't forget the unity and tripartite personality of God.

² Inc Merriam-Webster, *Merriam-Webster's Collegiate Dictionary*, Eleventh ed. (Springfield, MA: Merriam-Webster, Inc., 2003).

CHAPTER EIGHT

¹ John F. Walvoord, Roy B. Zuck and Dallas Theological Seminary, *The Bible Knowledge Commentary: An Exposition of the Scriptures*, (Wheaton, IL: Victor Books, 1983).

² Eusebius, Church History III.1.

CHAPTER NINE

[1] Tim Dowley, Ed., *Eerdmans' Handbook to the History of Christianity*, (Grand Rapids: Wm. B. Eerdmans Publishing), 436-442.

[2] "The Welsh Revival," http://www.welshrevival.com/lang-en/1904history.htm.

CHAPTER TEN

[1] Cited from Torrey's sermon, "Why God Used D. L. Moody," preached in 1923. See http://www.whatsaiththescripture.com/Voice/Why.God.Used.D.L.Moody.html.

CPSIA information can be obtained at www.ICGtesting.com
Printed in the USA
LVOW120350291112

309298LV00002B/5/P